Be Still

BE STILL

45 Days of Living in God's Stillness

Pastor Mark A. Gass

ISBN: 1507845421
ISBN 13: 9781507845424

Dedication

To my Daughters: Katie, Kimberly and Kayla. Every day I see in their lives different characteristics of their mother. May this book serve as a continual reminder of their mother's calm and confident faith in the midst of the storm. My prayer is that they continue in this faith.

Acknowledgements

Thanks to Valerie Bodden for editing and providing many valuable insights.

Special Thanks to Jane whose continual support encouraged me to bring this book to completion.

The quoted hymns are from CW (Christian Worship) and are Public Domain

Some verses are quoted from "Then Sings my Soul". Used by permission of Thomas Nelson Publishers

Prelude to the Journey

It was another one of those roller coaster days—the downhill drop of a roller coaster ride that never seems to end. Only yesterday, the doctor had begun to pull my wife Kris out of the medically induced coma she had been in since having brain surgery to remove a cancerous tumor a week ago. Now, as I sat in the family counseling room, listening to the doctor explain why he had to put Kris back under the coma, my heart plunged. There she lay—motionless—life in her body but no life to show us except the numbers on the monitor. Right outside this door was a waiting room filled with friends and family. How could I face them with the tears running down my face? "Stop it! Stop it!" I yelled inwardly to myself. "You are a pastor. You can't be crying. You are a pastor, and you must be strong." The more I rebuked myself, the more the tears came. Then those words hit me again—from my favorite Psalm—"Be still, and know that I am God." "Be still, and know that I am God." Take a deep breath. "Be still, and know that I am God." Wipe those tears from your eyes. "Be still, and know that I am God." Hold your hands steady. "Be still, and know that I am God." I am ready to speak to my friends and family once again. God is in control. "Be still." I am still as I reach for the doorknob and walk into the waiting room.

The Stillness of our God that comforted and consoled me on that difficult day remained with Kris and me throughout our experience with cancer. In fact, it became the most beautiful part of our journey. We were blessed with the opportunity to share the goodness, the love and the mercy of our God with an ever-widening circle of friends and relatives through daily e-mails. The God who spoke to our hearts, "Be still, and know that I am God," spoke to many other hearts through these messages.

Although our daily e-mail messages are shared throughout these devotions, ultimately, this book is not about Kris or me or you. This book is about the Lord and his unfailing promises and strength whatever the challenge in our lives. Even though this book centers on our journey of faith through our trials, it is also about your journey of faith and love. The sufferings that we share with you are meant only as an example of the Lord's continued guidance and his gracious hand of support. Our sufferings are by no means unique or the worst. Many people have commented about our struggles and how difficult they have been. The truth of the matter is that every person—including you—has or will face trials. When you do, it is my prayer that the promises of the Lord shared in this book will have given you more foundation for your life.

What is that foundation? Through this journey, there is one passage that has stood out at as the "theme passage" for my life. Psalm 46:10: "Be still, and know that I am God." The "stillness of God" refers to the peace, confidence and strength that we receive by trusting in the Lord Jesus as we journey through the challenges of life.

Our journey began many years ago. Some would say that it began in June 2000, when Kris was diagnosed with breast cancer. But really, this journey began way back in the Garden of Eden. When Adam and Eve first picked and ate of the fruit, turning their backs on their loving Creator, proceeding to follow their own will, sin flooded this world, and with it came all kinds of trials, weaknesses, illnesses and diseases. From that moment on, imperfection and sin served as impetus and gave rise to one disease and sickness after another. Out of this imperfection sprang the disease of cancer.

In 1992 and in 1994, Kris's two sisters died in their early forties of ovarian and breast cancer. Suspecting that this might be more than a coincidence, Kris underwent genetic counseling in 1995, and we learned that her family carried a genetic defect. All people carry tumor-suppressing genes. These are good genes. However, in many members of Kris's family, one of the two genes is defective. When the other one becomes defective too, cancer sets in. This genetic defect made Kris's chance of developing breast cancer rise from 30 percent for the average woman to 90 percent, while her ovarian cancer risk jumped from 7 percent to 35 percent.

Of course, it was not easy to learn of Kris's risk, and many medical professionals and others over the years asked us how we could live with this knowledge. Our response: "Be still, and know that I am God." Even in hard times, that remained the foundation of our lives. We knew that God was in control and we would deal with the disease when we had to deal with it—because God would deal with it for us!

The time to deal with it came in June 2000. Less than two weeks after burying my mother, Kris went in for her regular six-month examination as part of our precautionary testing. We were ready to leave when the radiologist stopped us. "We found something," she said. "Breast cancer." Words rammed into our hearts like gunshots. "Be still, and know that I am God." Several weeks later, surgery took place. Six weeks later, she was back at work. God is good.

For more than a year, Kris did well. Then, in September 2001, after she experienced several days of swollen legs, we visited our local doctor, who immediately set up a CAT scan, which showed cancerous spots all over her abdomen. The next day, we met with our oncologist and the surgeon, and within the week, Kris was entering the surgery room to remove the cancer. Although her ovaries had been taken out several years earlier, ovarian cancer had developed and mushroomed. It had invaded the uterus, several parts of the colon, the spine and part of the pancreas. Though the surgeon was hesitant to perform the surgery because he didn't think Kris would live long afterwards, he went ahead with the procedure. Six weeks later, Kris was home and working part time in between chemotherapy treatments. Be still—God is good.

A year and a half later, in March 2003, a spot was found by Kris's adrenal gland. Six months later, after treatments of oral chemo, all was fine.

Kris continued to receive regular checkups, and in early January 2004, her doctor found her to be in excellent health. Two weeks later, she began experiencing headaches. An MRI showed a tumor in her brain. Her ovarian cancer had metastasized to the brain. On February 11, she had surgery. She was joking that night. By February 14, she was up and walking. That night, her brain began to swell. At midnight, a nurse woke me from my sleep in the waiting room. She told me that they had to put Kris in a medically induced coma to alleviate the pressure on her brain. I was on my knees in the waiting room pleading before the Lord's throne when the doctor walked in to speak with me. So began our journey of hope and strength while Kris slept.

So began our journey…. So begins your journey of growing in the Stillness of the Lord.

Each day is divided into two sections: "Our Journey" and "Your Journey."

"Our Journey" follows the series of e-mails that I sent out each morning while Kris lay in her coma and then during her recovery and the months that followed. They are chronological in nature.

"Your Journey" follows a series of devotions based on the six words of Jesus from the cross. They are topical in nature.

To get the most out of your devotional reading, the author suggests that you follow this procedure:

1. Write down one or more challenges you are facing right now. This is what you will focus on as you read these devotions.
2. Begin with Day 1 and set aside the next 45 days to read one set of devotions a day, preferably early in the day to keep the passage for the day fresh in your mind. Each morning, take a few moments to read these devotions. Then read the Bible passage aloud five times. Throughout the day, speak this passage, and use it for quiet meditation while on a walk, in the car, at lunch break or making supper. You may be tempted to read ahead. Try to stick to one a day so that you can meditate on the thought for that day. Please note that a number of the stories and examples have been gathered over 23 years of ministry. These have been sources for devotions and sermons. The author or origin is not always known, but we have done our best to give credit for any known source. All Scripture passages are quoted from the New International Version.
3. Share this Bible passage with one person each day.
4. Find a devotional partner who will read along with you so that you can encourage each other to remain faithful as well as spend some time discussing the devotions.

It is my prayer that through the next 45 days, you will be led even more into the stillness of God.

So we begin—as we always should—in prayer:

Heavenly Father, I am about to embark upon a 45-day spiritual journey of meditation on your promises. Use these devotions to strengthen my soul and keep my eyes focused on your faithfulness. Help my devotion partner and myself to be committed to this journey. Dearest Jesus, gently take us by the hand every day and remind us that through each valley or mountain, you are with us. Holy Spirit, take your Word and open our hearts to understand and rest upon your good promises. Gracious God, speak to our souls in these devotions and remind us to "Be still, and know that you are God." Amen.

Week 1

Be Still in the Midst of Betrayal

The devotions for "Your Journey" will lead us from Jesus' words from the cross, "Father, forgive them, for they do not know what they are doing," to encourage us to Be Still even in the midst of betrayal.

DAY 1:

Our Journey

Wednesday, February 12, 2004

To all our wonderful friends in Jesus.

It is 11:30 p.m. on Wednesday evening, and I am typing from the hospital computer while Kris is resting comfortably in the ICU here at Theda Clark in Neenah. What wonderful blessings the Lord has showered our way this day! Our trip began yesterday as we left Tomahawk and stopped to see our good friend, Pastor Jim Wieland in Merrill, who shared a portion of God's Word with us and the Lord's Supper. He reminded us of God's promise in Isaiah 42 that we are engraved in the hand of our Savior God. We truly are. At every battle during this long war, the Lord has brought to our aid many good physicians. Yet, we know that these good physicians are guided by the hand of our Great Physician. In fact, the surgeon today told us he prays before each surgery. But, we have been bolstered not only by our Lord's many promises and his abiding presence, but by the many prayers of our wonderful friends. We thank you all. The surgery today was successful. The surgeon indicated that he has removed everything humanly possible. Kris came through the surgery "in an excellent way!" Surgery was finished about 3:30, and then a CAT scan about 5 indicated all normal. No neurological side effects from surgery. All functions normal. Up to ICU about 5:30, and then just about an hour ago she asked to sit up on the side of the bed. Although it made her a bit woozy, she accomplished it. Now she is resting. Tomorrow morning we will have another MRI, and then hopefully move to a regular room. We praise God for this first great step in defeating this battle. The doctor indicated that she should be released either Friday or Saturday. We will not see him for about 10 days, and then some time after that, she will have her first radiation treatment, which will require a hospital stay of about three days. This evening, one of the early visitors was a student from the Campus Ministry at the University of Oshkosh. Along with some wonderful flowers, there was a card signed by many of the students of the Campus House. I was truly humbled, and Kris and I are awed by your support and prayers. The card said, "'If you have faith as small as a mustard seed. Nothing will be impossible for you.' With your strength rooted in your faith, everything you attempt is guided by His hand." One student summed it up: "I will do the strongest thing I can for you: PRAY!" We are all truly engraved in the hand of our Savior, Jesus. Those same hands which stretched out so willingly on the cross are the same ones that carry us through the trials of life. Alright—it is late, and I am in the preaching mood, so I had better end. To all of you, whether we can personally speak to you or not, please be assured that we thank God for your love and concern and prayers. Please also keep the rest of Kris's family in your prayers. On this day, four family members were having surgery: Katie's grandfather Dick with knee surgery; Kris's brother-in-law Bill, with tailbone injury; and Kris's niece with surgery in New Orleans. Well, I am going to head back in for Kris's 12:00 hourly check. Nurses and doctors are a wonderful blessing, but it is nice to see a familiar face. You know Kris is doing OK when she was listing off all the things I need to tell the girls to do for school tomorrow. God's Blessings to all of you from both of us. Mark and Kris

DAY 1:

Your Journey

Psalm 46

[1]God is our refuge and strength, an ever-present help in trouble.
[2]Therefore we will not fear, though the earth give way and the mountains fall into the heart of the sea,
[3]though its waters roar and foam and the mountains quake with their surging.
[4]There is a river whose streams make glad the city of God, the holy place where the Most High dwells.
[5]God is within her, she will not fall; God will help her at break of day.
[6]Nations are in uproar, kingdoms fall; he lifts his voice, the earth melts.
[7]The Lord Almighty is with us; the God of Jacob is our fortress.
[8]Come and see the works of the Lord, the desolations he has brought on the earth.
[9]He makes wars cease to the ends of the earth; he breaks the bow and shatters the spear,
   he burns the shields with fire.
[10]"Be still, and know that I am God;
   I will be exalted among the nations, I will be exalted in the earth."
[11]The Lord Almighty is with us; the God of Jacob is our fortress.

This Psalm, which has become the theme of my life, is also the theme for the journey of faith we will take throughout these devotions. The writer begins the psalm with a great expression of confidence in the Lord. He is our refuge—our strength—our rock in the face of life's struggles. And those struggles can be great—mountains being thrown into the sea, nations in uproar—completely turning thousands of lives upside down within moments. We all have struggles that turn our own lives upside down, too. Yet, through them all, we can rest securely in the Lord's stillness. That stillness is found many places in Scripture to give us strength, encouragement and confidence to face each day.

The night before our Lord died, he gave us these beautiful words: "Do not let your hearts be troubled. Trust in God; trust also in me." You know what it means to have a troubled heart. A certain situation weighs on our hearts so much that we can feel it physically. Our heart may even hurt or feel like a huge weight is pressing down, threatening to flatten it. What is it that presses down on your heart? Is a loved one dying? Are you dying? Has a loved one died? Chemotherapy treatments wearing you down? You lost your job? Your children have left? Your spouse has left? Finances are threatened? Lost friends?

No matter what troubles you, it is my heartfelt prayer that you will take the challenge of this faith-renewing journey. During the next 45 days, the Lord would draw you to be still before him and his Word. His promise is certain that he will still your heart. What does this mean? Through his promise of love and forgiveness and hope, your troubled heart will have peace. Our hand is now on the door to this journey. Carried by the Lord's promise, enter this journey and "Be Still."

Be still, my soul; the Lord is on your side;
Bear patiently the cross of grief or pain;
Leave to your God to order and provide;
In every change, he faithful will remain.
Be still, my soul; your best, your heavenly friend
Through thorny ways leads to a joyful end. (CW 415)

DAY 2:

Our Journey

Friday, February 13, 2004

Good Morning Dear Friends in Christ,

We are still in the ICU here at Theda Clark and it is 5 a.m. on Friday, and I just came from visiting Kris. She is resting comfortably and seems to be a little more alert this morning. First, let me say this especially for my friends in Tomahawk. It seems that rumors have been circuiting in the Tomahawk area that Kris took a turn for the worse. This is not the case. Well, then what happened yesterday? Yesterday morning Kris's brain experienced some swelling. To a medical layman like me, this seemed like a setback. However, to the doctors this is part of the normal cycle. As the doctor said, "We are not surprised nor alarmed—just concerned.... Swelling is normal, but there is just a little more than what we would like to see." So, they began several new treatments. At the same time, Kris experienced nausea and head pain. Normal effects of surgery. All the medicine combined caused Kris to be very sleepy. But each time she still passed her neurological exams. But, visits to her were limited. My layman's mind has come to think of it this way: When Kimberly injured her knee and it swelled, what was the treatment—to rest it. When the brain swells, how do we rest it? Very little stimulation. So, we are limiting who and how long people visit with Kris. However, you know her. Several times she asked, "What should I do?" Just rest. To us who stand vigil by her side, we hurt to see her have to endure this trial. Kimberly and Kayla have come from Tomahawk so that we can be together and I can attend to their needs as well. While sitting in the chapel yesterday, the Bible was opened to Psalm 31: "In you, O Lord, I have taken refuge; let me never be put to shame; deliver me in your righteousness.... Be my rock of refuge, a strong fortress to save me." When I sit here alone, I have fled to my two favorite Psalms: 46 and 121. Those of you in

Tomahawk may know them well since I use them often as I visit with you. Today is a new day and his mercies are new every day. Sorrow is in the night but joy comes with the dawn of a new day. The Lord blessed me with five uninterrupted hours of sleep and has prepared me for the day to come. He has renewed my spirit, and let us all continue to turn to our Savior God, our great refuge and strength. To all in Tomahawk, I will have a further update for you this weekend in worship. Brothers and sisters, I have heard the roar of your prayers as they have ascended to the throne of grace, and I thank you for joining me before that throne. "God is our refuge and strength, an ever-present help in trouble. Therefore we will not fear, though the earth give way and the mountains fall into the heart of the sea, though it waters roar and foam.... **Be still, and know that I am God**.... The Lord Almighty is with us; the God of Jacob is our fortress." God's blessings, Mark

DAY 2:

Your Journey

"Be still, and know that I am God....
The LORD Almighty is with us; the God of Jacob is our fortress."
PSALM 46:10

We have entered through the door of this journey and here we stand. What lies before us? What lies before us is what lies as the foundation of our lives—the Lord's stillness. When God reveals himself to us, he shares his name with us—for the sole purpose of blessing and saving us. As God speaks to our hearts to be still, he does so on the basis of his name. Notice what he calls himself: the "LORD." In the NIV translation of the Bible, the word "LORD" in capital letters represents the Hebrew name for God: Jehovah or Yahweh. This word refers to God as the God of the Covenant. The covenant, or agreement, that God makes with his people is simply this: "I love you." He loves us so much that: "God so loved the world that he gave his one and only Son that whoever believes in him shall not perish but have eternal life." What a treasure this name is! In his name, our God reveals his care, devotion and love. In his name, we see our God, who saw Adam and Eve in their sin and disobedience and promised to send his Son. At the moment of our baptism, our God placed his name into our hearts. We are the Lord's, so we have the Lord in our heart. Having the Lord means having every blessing he won on the cross. Having the Lord means that the victory Christ won on the cross over Satan becomes our victory. Christ's hope becomes our hope. Christ's peace is our peace. Christ's joy is our joy.

When you get up from this devotion, you will be surrounded by the things you own. You are wearing clothes that you own. You are using things in your home, at work or at school that you own. Some of these possessions you value; others you don't think much about. Sometimes we try to find comfort in our possessions. During a blizzard, we find comfort in just being able to be home and sit still in our own easy chair. Why can we be still in the blizzards of life? We can be still because we have the greatest treasure in life—our LORD. Our Lord is not only in our hearts, but we live in him. He stands as that great fortress which no army can break through. His name stands as great walls of love that embrace us during days of sorrow, turmoil or crisis. What is your day going to be like? What storm will try to sweep into your heart? What problem threatens to swallow you like a sudden tsunami? Be still and know that you have the LORD and that he has you. Be still and know that all earthly possessions may be lost, but "nothing can separate you from the love of God that is in Christ Jesus." Be still and know the God of his covenant, the God of free and unlimited grace, has wrapped his arms of love around you, and nothing can rip you from his arms. Let your journey in God's promise today encourage your heart, reminding you of the thoughts of the hymnist:

Jesus, Jesus only Jesus, Can my heartfelt longing still!
Lo, I pledge myself to Jesus, What he wills alone to will,
For my heart, which he hath filled, Ever cries, "Lord, as thou wilt." (CW 348)

DAY 3:

Our Journey

Sunday, February 15, 2004

Dear Brothers and Sisters of Redeemer,

Since this past Wednesday, our lives have been on a roller coaster. Coming out of the surgery, Kris was doing great, but since then we have been up and down. Last night, Kris was really alert, and we thought that she was turning the corner. However, around midnight, she fell into a deep sleep, and she could not be aroused. The doctor decided to become proactive, and at 2 a.m., she was put into a medically induced coma to control her breathing as well as to allow her body the ability to relax and for the swelling to subside. Her condition has been listed as critical. I fervently seek your prayers. I have spent many moments alone in the hospital chapel reading the psalms and pleading with our Lord. He comforts us with his Word, but fears and tears still would invade. Our God is a gracious God, and we know his will is best. But, we still have the privilege to storm the throne of grace on behalf of Kris. The next 12-24 hours will be critical moments. I am comforted not only by my Lord but by the many prayers and thoughts of love that come from you. Thank you for your patience and support. I will update you as soon as I know more news. God's Blessings on your day. I will send updates via e-mail or even through WJJQ on Monday morning news time. Pastor and Kris Gass

DAY 3:

Your Journey

"So the sun stood still…. The Lord was fighting for Israel!"
Joshua 10:13-14

Every day is a day of grace, no matter what the battle. In Joshua 10, God's people are entering the Promised Land. But they are not unopposed—they must battle five kings from surrounding countries before they can take over the land God has promised them. Although God's people are winning the battle, night is coming. They need more time to chase the enemy army. They need light so that the enemy cannot escape into the darkness. Joshua prays for the Lord to still the sun so that the battle can be won. It is interesting to note that God's people were not being beaten. The enemy was present, but not victorious. Why? The Lord was fighting for Israel.

As I sat in the ICU when Kris was in her coma, life was stilled. We were engaged in a battle, but the Lord reminded us that our Savior had already fought and won for us. "Because he himself suffered when he was tempted, he is able to help those who are being tempted." Good Friday and Easter remind us that Satan has already been stilled. His power is broken. Sin's guilt has been removed. Death has no sting but is now the doorway to heaven. The Lord is fighting for us. In the midst of life's battles, nothing is too small or too big for our Lord.

What is your battle today? Disease? Loneliness? Anxiety? Financial concerns? Marriage concerns? Family concerns? Remember to enter each battle under the banner of the Lord's grace. "Be still, my soul; the Lord is on your side." He is on our side, as the song says, as our dearest friend. Our Savior Friend would remind us every morning to lay our problems on him and to rest in the stillness of his love. "Come unto me all you who are weary and burdened and I will give you rest," our Savior

Friend beckons to us. As you begin your day, whatever battle lies ahead, flee first of all to the arms of your Savior Friend.

What a friend we have in Jesus, All our sins and griefs to bear!
What a privilege to carry Everything to God in prayer!
Oh, what peace we often forfeit, Oh, what needless pain we bear,
All because we do not carry Everything to God in prayer! (CW 411)

DAY 4:

Our Journey

Monday, February 16, 2004

Good morning all,

I am still writing from my little "apartment" in the corner of the ICU waiting room at Theda Clark. Hope you don't mind my daily updates, but they are therapeutic for me. Took a walk to my car, and the crispness of the morning dawn reminded me that this is the first day of the rest of my life. With every new day, the Lord renews us with the rising of his Son in our hearts with his love and mercy. We have passed the first 24 hours without a major incident. Kris is resting comfortably and responding well to the medicine. Her brain pressure is remaining at "good" levels. Soon she will go for a CAT scan. As soon as that is done and I know that she is back in her room and set for the day, we are heading back to Tomahawk. I need to get the girls back home and ready for the week. Also, need to attend to some church business. Then coming back here late tonight or early tomorrow morning before they begin to take her off the respirator. We need to prepare for a much longer stay in the hospital. What had originally been a three- to four-day stay will now turn into at least a two-week stay. I cannot begin to express my gratitude for the outpouring of prayers and support from God's people. I thank God for you. My world has become this collection of chairs and couches in this 20x20 room. Your support and prayers have been a pipeline of love out of here. The Lord has seen fit to put us in this place, at this time, to serve his purposes. We don't always know what his purpose is, but we do know that God will sustain. One brother reminded me of the Lord's response to the apostle Paul: "My grace is made perfect in weakness." To whom should we turn but to our Lord who has in mind not to hurt us, but to save us. Have a great day in the Lord and remember to thank him for the ability to be in your own home and to walk and go about your business. It is day of grace to us. Mark and Kris

DAY 4:

Your Journey

"The Lord will fight for you; you need only to be still."
Exodus 14:14

Caught between a rock and a hard spot! We often feel that way. In the word before us today, God's people seemed caught. On one side was the Red Sea—and they had no boats. On the other side, the Egyptian army was bearing down on them. If they fled into the sea, many of them would be drowned. If they turned back to fight against the Egyptians, they would be shredded under the wheels of the chariots. God's people were in a panic. They grumbled and complained against their God. What were they to do? The answer may be surprising: nothing—absolutely nothing. Yes, that's right. God told his people to do nothing—to be still! God's stillness implies not that our God is still, but that we are still in our Lord's hands. "The Lord will fight for you; you need only to be still" was Moses' encouragement. In other words: Be quiet, sit down and just watch the Lord take care of it. You know well what the Lord did. Nearly two million people walked through the sea on dry land, arriving safely on the other side. Meanwhile, the Egyptian army was swallowed by the waters.

As we view our Lord's passion, we see the Lord's stillness—his calm and resolve—as he approached death. So we are to be quiet, sit down and just watch the Lord's suffering and death for us. What is our Red Sea? Who is our Egyptian army? Where are we stuck in life? Oftentimes, we find ourselves stuck because of sin in our lives. Sometimes sin lurks around, and we hold on to it because it seems fun. We harbor grudges, secretly hold onto sexual thoughts, find pleasure in drugs or alcohol, become entrapped in consistent lies or covet more possessions. When not resisted, sin and temptation will swallow us in a flood of evil consequences. Meanwhile, on the other side, things are there to attack us. The bill collector is at the door. Or the doctor shares some bad news.

Yet, God tells us to do the same thing he told his people to do at the Red Sea: Nothing! Just be still and watch him. Watch him as he carries the load of the cross. And remember that the weight that pressed down on his shoulders was not just the wooden cross; there was the unseen load as well. That unseen load included every load facing you right now. Whatever is weighing you down, remember that your Lord has already carried it. He already took care of it. In the face of an oncoming attack, be still as you sit down and watch our Lord doing battle on the cross. In the Garden, in the courtroom, on the cross, Satan was right there battling against our Lord. Yet, Jesus was victorious. He did not yell from the cross: "I am done." He rather shouted the cry of victory: "It is finished." Those words rose to the courts of heaven, bringing forth praise, and they struck despair to the very depths of hell. His victory is our victory. Today you will face battles and temptations. Take heart and rejoice. Sit down and be still—the Lord is fighting for you.

"Fear not, I am with you, Oh, be not dismayed,
For I am your God and will still give you aid;
I'll strengthen you, help you, and cause you to stand,
Upheld by my righteous, omnipotent hand." (CW 416)

DAY 5:

Our Journey

Wednesday, February 18, 2004

Morning of 2/18

Dear Friends in Christ,

All the doctors were in, and we had an encouraging update. The CAT scan today shows some reduction in the swelling. Although I am trying to get off this roller coaster and not get too excited or too down, I can't stop from thanking the Lord for this bit of good news. In addition, the nurse came up to me and was looking at a stack of cards and said, "I have to recheck this because I can't believe these could all be for you." Yes, they were. Taking my "long walk" back to the waiting room, I praised the Lord because, for the first time in a long time, my eyes were filled with tears of joy, for I held in my hands so many expressions of love from God's people. Thank you so very much. This morning's psalm—Ps. 3— reminded me: "To the Lord I cry aloud, and he answers me from his holy hill. I lie down and sleep; I wake again, because the Lord sustains me." Have a great day. Mark

Afternoon of 2/18

Dear Friends in Christ,

Let's try this again. The first one I sent this morning seemed to get lost in cyberspace. This is a challenge because the keys stick on this keyboard. Anyway, here it is a week later. Kris continues to be the same. We had a little scare Monday night because her brain pressure went up somewhat, but doctors assure us that all is fine for now. Last Saturday night, Kris was put into her medically induced coma and it appears she will be in this state for several days yet before they start bringing her out. But, I have stopped planning. I did have so many plans for my church, mission board and personal, but they are all set aside. Yet, I am reminded of our Lord's promise that his plans are not to harm us but to prosper us. After spending a day in Tomahawk, I am now here for the long haul. My church family is being very supportive and loving. I thank God for them and all my dear friends. One dear friend has offered to pay for a room at the Harbor House—a place like the Ronald McDonald house. So many have opened up their home, but I want to be as close as possible. As I take my "long walk," as I call it, from the waiting room to her room, I pray that one day I will turn the corner and hear Kris say, "Where have you been?" My response: on my knees before the Lord for you. Thanks for joining me there. I am getting frustrated with banging on this keyboard that only half works, so I am signing off. God's blessings to you this day. Thought for the day: If you are about to complain about something in your life today, stop and say a prayer. Have a great day. Mark and Kris

DAY 5:

Your Journey

"Be still before the Lord and wait patiently for him."
PSALM 37:7

Most of us aren't very good at waiting. It's just not a trait of our Western society. Fast food restaurants thrive not because the food is good, but because it is fast. When we wait more than two minutes in line at the grocery store, we complain. We expect turnaround answers to requests. If it takes someone longer than a day to return a phone call, we become impatient. We want it, and we want it now! Is this true of our attitude with God? We want our Lord to hear us and to hear us now—and we want our answer now! A good reading of the psalms shows us how to wait. The psalmist before us gives us the encouragement to wait in the stillness of the Lord.

The Hebrew word for "be still" is *dom*, from which our English word "dumb" (not able to speak) appears to be derived. The silence or stillness stands in contrast to grumbling or complaining. Psalm 37 speaks to one of the great ironies of life: "Why does it seem that the wicked prosper, while the righteous are afflicted?" When a believer enters upon hard times, he may be tempted to look around at others. "Why don't they suffer?" "Why do they keep their jobs and get raises, while I lose mine?" "Why do they have all the toys, while I struggle just to pay for the necessities?" "Why do they have the energy to enjoy the pleasures of life, while my health suffers to the point that I can't even go to church?" When days of sorrow overtake us, we are tempted to look over our shoulders and envy the life of others.

In John Bunyan's book *Pilgrim's Progress*, the characters Passion and Patience are a representation of the characters in Jesus' parable of the Prodigal Son. Both the youngest son in the Bible story and Passion in Bunyan's book yearned for the pleasures of life right now. They received the things they wanted but those things were soon gone. On the other hand, both the oldest son and Patience waited and received blessings that would never end. To be impatient with the problems of this life betrays in us the yearning of Passion. We want our good things, and we want them now. Yet, living in the stillness of the Lord brings us patience to wait for the "better things" that are to come—the blessings of life with Jesus here and in heaven. Later in this psalm we read, "Those the Lord blesses will inherit the land." The stillness of the Lord brings a sure and certain hope.

The writer ends this psalm with these words: "Consider the blameless, observe the upright; there is a future for the man of peace." Waiting in the stillness of the Lord implies a confidence in the future. Let us not become influenced by the world's desire to have the future now. Rather, let us consider the outcome of the way of peace—living in the Lord's stillness. At one man's funeral, the pastor put it this way: "Here is the Christian's way and his end, his motion, and his rest. His way is holiness, his end happiness; his motion is towards perfection and in uprightness; his peace is at his journey's end." This is a journey that shows us to wait in the stillness of the Lord's peace. Let this be our prayer:

> *Graciously my faith renew; Help me bear my crosses,*
> *Learning humbleness from you, Peace mid pain and losses.*
> *May I give you love for love! Hear me, O my Savior.*
> *That I may in heaven above Sing your praise forever. (CW 98)*

DAY 6:

Our Journey

Thursday, February 19, 2004

To my many dear friends in Christ,

Good morning from Theda Clark in Neenah, where God continues to surround Kris with his love and mercy. Things are about the same. God continues to be with us and provides strength for a new day. As one of my pastor friends shared with us last night from 1 John: "This is love: not that we loved God, but that he loved us and sent his Son as an atoning sacrifice for our sins." Love—that is Jesus—never fails, but is new every morning. Kris continues to be in the medically induced coma, and her numbers continue to be "good" for the state that she is in. Once again, the doctor reminds us that this is a bumpy ride and we just have to ride it out. Meanwhile, we stand vigil, continuing to pray. I thank all those who have sent words of love or have stopped by— especially the number of pastors who stopped in. This has proved to be a testimony to the other families. You have all thought so much of Kris and our family, but I would also today encourage your prayers for Kris's mother. She also stands vigil with us. I have not even begun to experience the sorrow and loss that she has faced in her life on this earth. Yet, what she has lost, the Lord has given back to her in strength of will and devotion to prayer. She is an inspiration to the rest of us as one "constant in prayer"— even in the car. However, we encouraged her not to fold her hands while driving the car! Kris truly loves her mother and was more worried about how she would take this news than us when this all came down. But, we sit and pray and stand vigil and, yes, even laugh. As one other pastor reminded us last night from Philippians, we are to rejoice in all things and give thanks and do not be anxious but present our requests to God. So that is what we do. Yesterday, we began our journal of love, with every visitor writing their notes of encouragement, and I can't wait to share it with Kris when she awakens. Wonderful thoughts. Could tomorrow be the day that the doctor begins to bring Kris out of this "sleep of healing"? I don't know and have stopped looking forward. Today, God will give us what we need, and then we will face tomorrow when it comes. Today, let us keep our eyes on Jesus, the author and perfector of our faith. God's Blessings. Mark and Kris

DAY 6:

Your Journey

"Father, forgive them, for they do not know what they are doing."
LUKE 23:34

There once was a Princess Alice in England. Her little daughter was critically ill with diphtheria. The doctor forbade her to kiss the little girl, lest she also contract the disease. In one of the girl's spells of delirium, the mother picked up the girl, pressed her to her bosom and soothed her. When the little girl regained consciousness, she sobbed: "Mother, kiss me." Without stopping to think what it might cost, the princess kissed her daughter. Before many days passed, the child had recovered, but the mother was dead. A mother's love runs deep—but our Savior's love runs even deeper. Even when we didn't ask to be kissed, our Savior gave us the kiss of forgiveness.

In the face of trial, we can be still in the Lord because we are stilled by his kiss of love. "Father, forgive them." The words almost knock us over. What would we do if we were being sentenced to death unjustly? What would our last words be? Words of vengeance and anger? Words of cursing and rage? None of these were to be found on the lips of our Savior. No—Jesus, in his human state, lived in the Lord's stillness. He did not complain or retaliate.

What happens to us when we hear these words? What impact do they have on our heart? In an art gallery, a man stood for a long time gazing at a picture of the crucified Savior. In the midst of all the hustle of those scurrying around him, he sighed aloud: "I love Him, my Savior." Another man, standing close by heard this and also said, "I love him, too." Before long, many others were all standing there looking at the crucified Savior in stillness.

As we view the grace of our Savior and hear him pray, "Father, forgive them for they know not what they do," are we not also led to say, "I love Him, too, my Savior"? To be still and to wait patiently comes from a heart of love. As the favorite Sunday school passage states: "We love because he first loved us." With the hymnist we sing:

O the height of Jesus' love!
Higher than the heavens above.
Deeper than the depths of sea,
Lasting as eternity.
Love that found me – wondrous thought! –
Found me when I sought him not (CW 385)

DAY 7:

Our Journey

Friday, February 20, 2004

Good Morning.

It is Friday morning, and we have entered Day Nine—nine days of God's goodness and grace. Nine days of his strong arm upholding us. The weather outside is pretty dreary, but we are beginning today with a little of the Sonshine of God's enduring hope. Last night, the doctor and I had a longer talk. Even though these surgeons are excellent doctors, they are always in a hurry. But, last night we had a few moments. As he has in the past, he just reassured me that all is going along just fine. Each brain reacts differently, and so we just have to take it day by day. There was a lot of compression from the tumor, and it just is taking time for everything to work its way back into place and to reconnect. How wondrous God has made us, and how mysterious is this mass of tissue that controls our body! Even the best doctor does not know completely the marvelous workings of the brain, but the Creator knows. We rest in his hands. The doctor feels that we are very close to turning the corner. But he cannot predict when. God knows when, and he will reveal it to us in due time. Until then, we stand vigil beside Kris as she rests in healing sleep. I am thankful for God's love and God's people and my dear friends who visit me and get me out of here from time to time. I often feel that it is unfair that we should receive all this encouragement when I look around at others who do not have that encouragement. There are now 13 people in CCU [Critical Care Unit], and I have seen precious few pastors visiting them, while Kris and I continue to be ministered to daily. We begin this day with our Lord saying: "Never will I leave you nor forsake you." Mark and Kris

DAY 7:

Your Journey

"Lord, do not hold this sin against them."
ACTS 7:60

The art of love and forgiveness must be learned, not by our own might or reasoning, but at the foot of the cross. It was there that Stephen obtained the strength to pray this prayer of forgiveness for those who were stoning him, even as his life was slipping away.

How his prayer stands in dark contrast to the attitude that often fills our lives! Even though we speak of love, how hard it is to practice what we preach. We are tempted to repay evil with evil. Our sinful nature is inclined to hold a grudge rather than to forgive those who have done us harm. Some people even let such flimsy little things as hurt feelings keep them from church and from the Lord's Supper. Consider Jesus—he had much more than hurt feelings when he offered his prayer, "Father, forgive them." Stephen was suffering more than just a little ridicule when he spoke in love: "Do not hold this sin against them."

Devotional journeys are a time of heart cleaning. How clean is your heart? Did your parents mistreat you? Did your grown children neglect you? Did your brothers and sisters malign or cheat you? Did someone slander or insult you? Did your pastor or church officer hurt you? Has your husband or wife misused you? Have you suffered any kind of injury? As long as we are sinners living among sinners, we ought to expect others to sin against us from time to time. Since we aren't perfect, why should we expect others to be perfect? Yet, when we flee to the foot of the cross and see the dying Savior utter his words of love, we are strengthened in our resolve to love others even when they hurt us.

A loveless life is like a living death. One man put it this way: "He who refuses to forgive others breaks the bridge over which he himself must pass to reach heaven." When you find it difficult to love, to forgive, then hurry in spirit to Calvary and kneel and listen to your Savior. Be enveloped in the stillness of the Lord as he calmly cries from the cross: "Father, forgive them for they do not know what they are doing." When you do this, remember that he is not just praying for all those people gathered at the cross; he is praying for you. The night before our Savior died, Jesus called us to live by a new command: "A new command I give you: Love one another. As I have loved you, so you must love one another. By this all men will know that you are my disciples, if you love one another." (John 13: 34-35)

> *O God of mercy, God of might, In love and mercy infinite,*
> *Teach us, as ever in your sight, To live our lives to you.*
>
> *You sent your Son for all to die That fallen man might live thereby.*
> *Oh, hear us, for to you we cry In hope, O Lord, to you.*
>
> *Teach us the lesson Jesus taught: To feel for those his blood has bought,*
> *That ev'ry deed and word and thought May work a work for you.*
>
> *(CW 499)*

Week 2

Be Still in the Midst of Hopelessness

The devotions for "Your Journey" will lead us from Jesus' words from the cross, "Today you will be with me in paradise" to encourage us to Be Still even when everything seems hopeless.

DAY 8:

Our Journey

Saturday, February 21, 2004

Dear Friends in Christ,

Good Morning! At Theda Clark here in Neenah, the sun is shining through after a snowy day. I was going to write after results of this morning's CAT scan, but today is Saturday, and things may run slower. I wish I could tell you something has improved, but we are still in our holding pattern. Last night Kris's numbers even shot up a little, but this morning when I walked in, they were coming down. However, she doesn't like to be moved, so the trip to the CAT scan caused some elevation in her numbers. Every morning when I walk over here from the Harbor House, I ask the Lord what kind of day is this going to be. The answer—it is always good because our Lord is a good and gracious God who promises to never leave or forsake us. Last night, I sat with Kris for quite a while and read the Psalms with her and spoke as if she were praying these psalms to her Lord. These wonderful words from Scripture take us through the emotions of the human heart and lead us to the security and safety of our Lord. I even have a chance to do some ministry here. I have been talking with a family whose mother was hit by a truck. Today, they are going to take her off of life support, and she probably will not have long to live. I have been able to join them around her bed to share God's Word, and they have asked me today to be with them when this happens. Another family is walking the same kind of path that we are, and I am able to give them some insights from our experience and so we all comfort and encourage each other. Our Lord reminds us to seize every opportunity to share Law and Gospel, for these are the words of eternal life. From our CCU hearts to yours, may your day be filled with the promises of God's love. Tomorrow is Sunday—let it truly be the Lord's Day! Mark and Kris

DAY 8:

Your Journey

"I tell you the truth, today you will be with me in paradise."
LUKE 23:43

One of the lessons that I learned while visiting with people at the ICU when Kris was hospitalized is the value of hope. I have looked into the eyes of many people hurting and grieving. I have seen the eyes of many who have lost a loved one. What a joy to see eyes filled with hope even though tears may be pouring out in great sorrow. But, what sadness to see those eyes vacant of hope.

Today, our attention will be turned to the thief on the cross and his plea to Jesus, "Jesus, remember me when you come into your kingdom." In the last hours of his life, this man had found God's stillness. We do not know much about the repentant thief, but obviously he had committed crimes that warranted the most severe punishment. Yet, his greatest sin was that for most of his life he had trusted in himself and felt no need for Jesus. How often we have been guilty of the same sin, as manifested by our lukewarm prayers at home and church or by trusting in ourselves rather than our Savior.

Yet, walking through this journey reminds us that we need not live in hopelessness. When the thief approached the cross, he did not have much hope. He joined with those in the crowd who were cursing and swearing and ridiculing Jesus. But look what changed him! He heard the words of love. He saw the calmness and stillness of Jesus. The Lord took hold of his heart and began to fill it first with love and then hope.

Having completed one week of our journey, the Lord would also take hold of your heart. Where does he find it? Is your heart in the midst of great sorrow? Is it broken?

Stressed? In crisis? Is your heart leaping at good news of recent blessings? Whatever the condition of our heart, we can flee to the foot of the cross. What irony! Looking up at a dying man, we see eternal life. Viewing a dying Savior brings an abundance of hope, as we see the doors of heaven flung open for the thief and for us: **"I tell you the truth, today you will be with me in paradise."**

Jesus sinners does receive;
Oh, may all this saying ponder
Who in sin's delusions live
And from God and heaven wander.
Here is hope for all who grieve—
Jesus sinners does receive. (CW 304)

DAY 9:

Our Journey

Sunday, February 22, 2004

Dear Friends in Christ,

Good Morning from Theda Clark! It has been one week since Kris went to sleep. This week has been slow and fast at the same time. Slow in that Kris has not awoken, but fast in that one week has already gone by that we have not been able to spend with family and friends. I appreciate the many cards of encouragement, e-mails and those stopping by. You have spoken of our faith, and sometimes I feel like you don't know me—my innermost thoughts, my times of doubt and anger. Yesterday morning, we had received some good news that the CAT scan showed a little less swelling. But that news was clouded by the fact that Kris's numbers of her brain pressure kept jumping up and down and in fact, jumping fairly high into the 40s. Despite the good news, I felt like I was getting to my lowest. I fled to the hospital chapel, which has become my sanctuary, and with the Psalmists literally called out to God, "How long, O Lord, will you shut up the doors of heaven? How long will you stay behind closed doors and not show your face? It is time to act, O Lord. It is time to sweep down from the heavens and touch the head of Kris with your healing hand." Even as I spoke those words, the answer was there. Looking at the cross of Christ, I knew he had not hidden his face. He was not behind closed doors. He had once left his throne, and with his healing hands, he placed them on the cross for us and still is with us. Yesterday afternoon, my youngest daughter (7 years old) brought a poster which her class had made. All of the 1st graders' pictures were on it in the shape of angels. It said, "First Grade Angels are watching over you." I know God doesn't work through posters, but after I hung that poster in the hallway outside her door, Kris's numbers began to come down. And they came down and they came down. They had been all day, but we hadn't seen it because our eyes were clouded with our own frustration. For the last 12 hours plus, Kris has been below 10!!!!! Praise be to the Lord to whom I have consistently prayed that his angels would surround the bed of the mother of our three children. My joy is tempered because I don't want to get too high and then come down. However, my good friend Tony reminded me not be like a typical pastor and not show joy. With those words of advice, I would sing from the rooftop of this hospital of the Lord's great love and mercy. This by no means is the end of our trial. Yet, when we are at our lowest, God shines on us. We still have a long ways to go and many battles to face and mountains to climb. But, today, we will go to God's house and rejoice in the green pasture of his blessings today. Ok—I have written more than I should, and it is Sunday and I had to preach my sermon somewhere, since we are not back in our beloved Redeemer Church. God's Blessings to all of you today. Thank you for your prayers, and I pray that all of you will find a place of worship today so that your soul may be strengthened by the preaching and teaching of His Word. Mark and Kris

DAY 9:

Your Journey

"Hope deferred makes the heart sick, but a
longing fulfilled is a tree of life."
PROVERBS 13:12

Webster's dictionary defines hope as "to desire with expectation of fulfillment." At first glance, the definition of that word seems to imply that hope
is a guarantee of the future. However, in our Western American society,
the use of the word "hope" does not necessarily imply that something is a certainty.
"I hope the Packers win." "I hope the sun will come out." As we commonly use this
word, it indicates a wish, but not a sure fact.

As the writer of Proverbs says: Hope deferred, or hopelessness, makes the heart
sick. In this case, we are talking about spiritual health. What makes a person spiritually healthy is continuing to feast on the banquet of Christ's promises. Christ's promises nourish our souls and prepare us for the days ahead. The teacher in Ecclesiastes
tells us in chapter 12: "Remember your Creator in the days of your youth, before the
days of trouble come." We remember our Creator when we feast upon and partake
of the many good and gracious promises from our Savior. Those promises assure us
that our Lord has become our Savior. These promises keep us calm amidst the storms
and trials of life. Amidst all of the panic aboard the *Lusitania* when it was going down,
a Christian man stood calm and still. "This shall be the greatest thrill of my life," he
was heard to exclaim as his body was about to be overtaken by the cold Atlantic waves.
That man had hope. He had a desire—a desire to go home to heaven, and he expected
it to be fulfilled. Why? Because the Lord had said so.

Yet, how many lie in hopelessness! How many have nothing to grasp! Why? They
did not take the time to be nourished by the Lord's promises. Their lives are too busy,

too preoccupied with the things of this world. Instead of devoting time for worship and spiritual nourishment, they spend their weekends skiing, or camping, or hunting, or relaxing at home in bed. While increasing the delights of their bodies and receiving their temporary happiness, they are starving their souls. Christians, too, can feel this hopelessness when they fall to the temptation to take their eyes off of Jesus.

This journey of meditation is a great time to be nourished. As you and I view the suffering and death of our Lord, we realize first of all that we have hope. We have a sure and living hope—not a maybe thing. Hopelessness comes when people try to hold onto things that have no substance or foundation. Yet, every time we gather in worship, every Sunday at the Lord's table, every day as we take a few moments in his word, we are eating of the tree of life, and our hope is strengthened. Stand firm because you know this important truth:

> *My hope is built on nothing less*
> *Than Jesus' blood and righteousness;*
> *I dare to make no other claim*
> *But wholly lean on Jesus' name.*
> *On Christ, the solid rock, I stand;*
> *All other ground is sinking sand. (CW 382)*

DAY 10:

Our Journey

Monday, February 23, 2004

Dear Friends in Christ,

Monday morning—The beginning of a new week here in Theda Clark in Neenah. Good Morning. It has now been over 36 hours since Kris's brain pressure (ICP—InterCranial Pressure) has been consistently 10 and under. The major sedative that was used to put her into a deep sleep has been taken off, while others remain. We continue to take one step forward toward the day that Kris will wake up again and return to us. What kind of day is this going to be? What kind of week? I have stopped guessing and just live for the good news of the moment. It could be Wednesday or Thursday before we see any visible reaction from Kris, but again, whenever the Lord chooses. Last evening, one of my dear friends who works in the area of Hispanic outreach visited me. He encouraged me with the words from the Spanish Bible from the account of the apostle Paul. Paul had his "thorn in the flesh," and three times he asked God to take it away. God's response? "My grace is sufficient for you." The Spanish word for sufficient has the meaning of "more than enough." How true. Maybe we think we have "enough" grace. No—we have "more than enough." He heaps it upon us in abounding measures. What kind of day or week will it be for you? Will you have problems at work, the car break down, the children get sick, the computer break, someone get injured, struggle with homework, struggle with your spouse, struggle with your friend, wonder how to pay the bills.... I know that whatever Kris and the girls and I face this week, we will have more than enough grace—God's undeserved love. This love is so evident as we prepare for Ash Wednesday. This Wednesday, many Christians will begin the tradition of attending midweek worship. For my church in particular, I have often commented that the most important part of midweek worship is the reading of the "Passion"—the suffering and death of Christ. A thousand sermons could be spoken, but nothing is better than the simple words of the true account of how our Lord took his steps to the cross, to the grave and to the empty tomb for us. This is grace. This is what propels us every day. Alright—I'll stop. Someone commented that I must be going through preaching withdrawal since I haven't been in my beloved Redeemer family for quite some time. Today is a good day at Theda Clark not just because of the numbers but because of God's grace. I pray that today is a good day for you, too—no matter what you face—you have "more than enough grace." Thank you to all for your cards, e-mails and visits of encouragement. I am saving them all, and Kris will read them during her time of recovery, and they will be a source of encouragement. God's Blessings. From our CCU hearts to yours. Mark and Kris

DAY 10:

Your Journey

**"Put your hope in God, for I will yet praise
him, my Savior and my God."**
PSALMS 42:5

Holy Scripture does not tell us who wrote Psalm 42, but it certainly carries the same tone and theme of King David's other psalms. In this psalm, we see a great example of how the Christian can speak to his own soul. Often I would speak God's Word to myself to calm my troubled soul. This self-encouragement is seen throughout Scripture, especially in the psalms of David. "Why are you downcast, O my soul?" David asks himself. As he asks, he uses the promises of God to lift himself up. In his depression, David was like many of the "greats" in human history. Churchill described depression and hopelessness as a "black dog" that followed him around. Charles Spurgeon, an extremely moving preacher, suffered from depression due to extreme pain from the gout. Martin Luther also suffered with depression. Do you? We all do from time to time. Some people are more prone to depression or a sense of hopelessness than others. What is it that gets you down? Is it physical pain? Or maybe a loss or a serious conflict or trial?

There was a man who once said, "hope never affords more joy than in affliction." It is only through the rain that the sun produces its beautiful rainbow. Through the raindrops of trial and sorrow, the Son of God produces his beautiful rainbow of hope. How does our God produce hope? Notice what the psalmist says—"for I will yet praise him, my Savior and my God." Hopelessness oftentimes results from navelgazing. We look at our own problems, our own trials and sufferings. Praise lifts our eyes from the temporary troubles to the good and gracious promises of our God. The psalmist calls him "my Savior." He uses the pronoun "my." At this very intense moment of his life, he sees God not as the grand Savior of all or the architect of the world's salvation. No, this is *my* God. He is here for me. All is not lost, because my Savior came to find me—the lost one!

Hopelessness and despair often come from a heart that believes that if God isn't dead, at least his promises are. Christian faith and hope tell us the opposite. The resurrection of our Savior proves that the promises of our Lord are alive and sure. Throw off the shackles of hopelessness by lifting your eyes in praise today. God encourages you not to be wrapped up in your problems and troubles, but to keep your eye on—and put your hope in—your Savior, your God.

Helen Lemmel was born into a minister's family and married a wealthy businessman, who left her when she became blind. Living in poverty and suffering from severe headaches, she nevertheless lived in the great stillness of the Lord's hope, dictating this great hymn:

> *O soul, are you weary and troubled? No light in the darkness you see?*
> *There's light for a look at the Savior, And life more abundant and free!*
>
> *Turn your eyes upon Jesus, Look full in his wonderful face,*
> *And the things of earth will grow strangely dim, in the light of His glory and grace!*
>
> *("Turn Your Eyes Upon Jesus" from Songbook: <u>Then Sings My Soul</u>)*

DAY 11:

Our Journey

Tuesday, February 24, 2004

Dear Friends in Christ,

Good Morning from Theda Clark! No—nothing is wrong. I know my daily update is late, but I just changed my routine this morning. My sister-in-law told me that Kris won't recognize me when she wakes up and sees my extra poundage from just sitting around, so I thought that I better get out and run. I need to add physical exercise to my spiritual exercising. While running, I was contemplating the journal that we have started. We have a journal that I entitled: "To Kris, While you were sleeping— A Journal of Our Vigil of Love for You." Every visitor signs in with a message. They are truly unique, and I can't wait until I can show Kris. Today all continues to be the same. Kris's numbers are staying low, and one more medicine is being reduced today. It is becoming even more apparent to me that waking up Kris will be a much longer process. But if that is what it takes, so be it. Not much else to report except that today is Fat Tuesday, which means tomorrow is Ash Wednesday. Here is my personal encouragement to all of my dear friends: Lent is my favorite time of the year. Especially during midweek Lenten meditations, the best thing we do is review the Passion of our Lord and Savior. If you have not yet made the commitment to be in worship, do so. I can guarantee this because it is the Lord's promise: if you spend the next 40 days in consistent worship both on Sundays and Wednesdays, your faith will be strengthened and your appreciation for your Lord's Passion will be magnified, which will result in the blessings of peace, love and hope in your life. To all my pastor friends, don't get stressed out over all the extra services. Take time yourself to enjoy your Lenten journey, and as I always say to you: "Have fun because we are in the best calling." God's Blessings to all of you on your Lenten journey. Mark and Kris

DAY 11:

Your Journey

**"But the eyes of the Lord are on those who fear him,
on those whose hope is in his unfailing love."**
PSALM 33:18

The eye of the Lord is on everything that happens in this world. Nothing escapes his notice, and nothing happens without his permission. This point is driven home by the illustration just before this verse: "No king is saved by the size of his army; no warrior escapes by his great strength. A horse is a vain hope for deliverance; despite all its great strength it cannot save." God is a sure hope, while a horse—a symbol of man's strength—is a vain hope. It is an empty, hollow strength that will give way. Many kings have risen to great heights, but when the decree of heaven goes out, the mighty kings fall. At the battle of Arbela, in 331 B.C. the Persian army numbered between 500,000 and 1 million men, but it was completely routed by Alexander the Great's army of 50,000. Napoleon led more than half a million men into Russia, but after one winter, they were a devastated group, and soon Napoleon was a prisoner. How many people have tried to put their hope in their own strength, their own wisdom, their own ability, only to be defeated or brought low? Many of the mightiest men of this world now call hell their eternal home. Nothing they did, nothing they devised with their own intelligence could they give to God to earn their salvation. The eyes of the Lord wanted to look on them but their pride rejected his love. They trusted only in themselves. But those who put their hope in the Lord can trust that his eye looks upon them with unfailing love.

Consider this example. The sun shines upon the whole world and provides heat and light. But take a magnifying glass and concentrate the beam of light on a piece of paper and it will set fire to the paper. God, in his providence, looks with general care upon his entire creation. But when he shines down with the beam of his love upon a believer, that person's heart burns with forgiveness and mercy and hope.

Later in this psalm the writer says, "We wait in hope for the Lord; he is our help and our shield." During a storm at sea, while most of the passengers aboard a ship were frantic and running about, one young man was not only at peace but actually merry. "How can you be happy and peaceful at a time like this?" he was asked. To this, in faith and hope, he responded that the pilot of the ship was his father and he knew that his father would take care of him.

The great and wise God, who is our Father, has from the beginning of time determined the events of the world and our life. He is the pilot sitting at the stern of our life. Even when the ship of the church or of the state or of our lives is sinking, we can be of good comfort because he will take care of us.

Jesus, Savior, pilot me
Over life's tempestuous sea;
Unknown waves before me roll,
Hiding rock and treacherous shoal.
Chart and compass come from thee:
Jesus, Savior, pilot me. (CW 433)

DAY 12:

Our Journey

Wednesday, February 25, 2004

Dear Friends in Christ,

Good Morning and God's Blessings to you on this Ash Wednesday. Yesterday I was reminded of a discussion I had many years ago in a pastor's study group. One of my friends came and read Isaiah 53. It was then that I remembered that in our study group many years ago, we talked about whether Isaiah 53 refers not only to spiritual problems but also to physical problems, especially when it says, "He took up our infirmities and carried our sorrows." It is right to say that Isaiah 53 (and I would suggest that you read and think of the suffering of Christ) speaks mainly to our spiritual problems. Today I am reminded that each and every sin that Kris, my children and I have committed is washed clean, taken care of and forgiven by our Lord and Savior. That is the main message of Lent and Ash Wednesday. However, in Matthew 8:17, this section from Isaiah 53 is also quoted as it finds fulfillment in the healings of Jesus. It is also right to say that Jesus suffered for our physical problems as well. And so, in my evening devotion with Kris and several of my friends last evening, we shared this. It doesn't mean that God will necessarily take away every disease, but his strength will get us through it, and his love will sustain us. It also means, as so many have reminded me, that this suffering is not God's punishment on us but rather God would work through this to the glory and blessing of his people. With this confidence, I begin the Lenten season. Many of my friends are busy today with the last touches on their sermons and services, but today I will be a hearer of his Word, letting others minister to me. I am thankful for all those, both pastors and friends, who have served Kris and me with the Word either through personal presence, letter or e-mail. Kris

48

continues to do well. Several medicines have been removed or greatly reduced, and her numbers and vitals stay good. After the CAT scan today, I pray that the doctor will say that today is the day that we begin the long process of waking her up. But if not today, then tomorrow, and I have learned to take one day at a time—believe me, that is hard for a pastor. Every day I look to the cross and the empty tomb and remember the many promises of our Savior. To all our dear friends, Kris and I both wish you a faith-inspiring Lenten season. May these next 40 days find you taking moments to reflect on the "Passion of Christ." Mark and Kris

DAY 12:

Your Journey

"I wait for the Lord, my soul waits, and in his word I put my hope."
PSALM 130:5

Anyone who has spent some time in the hospital knows that each day the most watched for visit is the visit from the doctor. Most doctors make their rounds early in the morning. While standing vigil over my wife during her 22-day coma, my daily routine was simple. Living next to the hospital in a hospital house, I would awaken around 5 a.m. After showering and cleaning up the place, I would head over to the ICU. After checking in on Kris and offering prayer, I would head down to get a quick breakfast and then back up to the ICU to wait for the doctor, who would arrive any time between 6:30 and 8:00 a.m. How I waited for the doctor to come in to hear any word—any word of hope or encouragement. Even though for many days the word was the same, it was good to hear it right from the doctor's mouth rather than from the nurses. After all, he was in charge.

More importantly, are we not encouraged to hear a word of hope or consolation from our Lord? In the stillness of the early hours of the hospital, we waited for the doctor's words. Living in the stillness of the Lord's mercy, how much more don't we wait for the Lord's word. After all, he is in charge.

The psalmist in this verse speaks of putting hope in the Lord's Word. What a great attitude to have! This hope does not disappoint us. This hope finds its fulfillment at the cross and at the empty tomb. Gazing up at the cross, we see Jesus fulfilling the promise given to Adam and Eve and to so many generations that followed. Peering into the empty tomb, we see the Father accepting the sacrifice of Jesus and throwing his blessings out for all mankind.

The source of our hope is the Lord. Our Lord comes to us in his word. Do you need some words of encouragement today? As you face trial or suffering or challenge, are you looking for something to hold onto—something to grasp? Put your hope in the word—the word of the Lord. Take the precious book that he has given to you and dig into his word. God is not hidden to us. He is right there in the Bible. In those beautiful words are found the best medicine for hopelessness, the best antidote to depression and the healing salve for any harm in life. This word gives us a foundation for life that never gives way. Stand on it and see if you are not comforted with the only hope that is sure and living, as the hymnist declares:

How firm a foundation, O saints of the Lord, Is laid for your faith in his excellent Word! What more can he say than to you he has said, Who unto the Savior for refuge have fled?

"Fear not, I am with you. Oh, be not dismayed, For I am thy God and will still give you aid; I'll strengthen you, help you, and cause you to stand, Upheld by my righteous, omnipotent hand." (CW 416)

DAY 13:

Our Journey

Thursday, February 26, 2004

Dear Friends in Christ,

Good Morning from Theda Clark. I have to say two things in this e-mail. One concerning Kris and another about my congregation. First of all, about Kris: She is completely off the paralyzing drug and has shown a few movements to the nurse. She still is under sedation, and when the doctor comes in this morning, he may or may not say to start backing off on the sedation. It all depends on her brain pressure numbers. Otherwise, she is doing fine. Secondly, concerning my congregation. The apostle Paul once said to his beloved Philippians: "If you have any encouragement from being united with Christ, if any comfort from his love, if any fellowship with the Spirit, if any tenderness and compassion, then make my joy complete by being like-minded, having the same love, being one in spirit and purpose." (Philippians 2:1-2) As a pastor, my joy is first and foremost in the Lord and his Passion for us, as with all of us as Christians. But, God gives pastors a special joy when God's people are responding to the word. I say this not with pride but with all humility and thankfulness to God's people. Being gone from my flock, I still am concerned for them. But they have added to my joy by their messages of love and support for Kris and me. Then, they furthered my joy by packing God's house last night even in my absence. As the apostle Paul said, "I thank my God every time I remember you.... I always pray with joy because of your partnership in the gospel from the first day until now." We truly have become partners, and for that I am thankful. As I write this e-mail this morning, I pause to pray for all of you that today you can pray with joy no matter what the situation in life. May God our Father surround your life today with the love of Jesus and the joy of knowing that you through faith rest in his goodness. God's blessings. Mark and Kris

DAY 13:

Your Journey

"We have this hope as an anchor for the soul, firm and secure."
Hebrews 6:19

When I was a boy, I went fishing a lot more than I do now. Although we never had a boat, we found ways to fish, usually along the shoreline. However, a family friend once offered to let me use his boat any time I wanted to fish on Lake Winnebago in east-central Wisconsin. Being adventurous, I set out one morning by myself. The water was a little rough, but my friend had equipped the boat with all the necessary provisions, including an anchor. Making my way out to the lake, I took notice of where the others fishermen were heading. I picked a spot and dropped anchor. I barely had my line in the water when I noticed that I was drifting near some other boats. I pulled up the anchor, started the motor and moved away. Soon after dropping my line back in the water, I noticed that I was again drifting toward the other boats. What was wrong? Why wasn't the anchor holding? Sure, it was a strong wind, but the anchor should hold. And then I realized: the anchor could hold only if the rope was long enough to reach the bottom. My friend had given me too short a rope. The anchor was useless—and at that moment, I felt like my friend was useless too.

What a blessing that we don't have to feel that way about our God. In the verse immediately preceding this one, we read: "it is impossible for God to lie, we who have fled to take hold of the hope offered to us may be greatly encouraged." How often in my sermons I repeat the phrase: God is not a man that he should lie. People lie to us all the time. Politicians exaggerate the truth to get elected. The media tells one side of the truth for ratings. Coworkers withhold the truth for their own advancement. Friends often betray the truth just for the fun of it. Spouses tell only what is necessary to keep things smooth. But in the end, it is all lies. In the movie *Liar, Liar*, a boy's birthday wish is that his dad cannot lie—ever. The subsequent plot shows how often people are expected to lie and the trouble they face when they don't.

But God does not lie. When he speaks of salvation, he is not exaggerating the truth. When he lays out his plan of grace, he does not tell one side of the truth or withhold portions of the truth. God's Word does tell us everything that our Savior has accomplished to make peace between God and man. All the good and gracious promises of our Savior are like an anchor that is sunk deep into the rock of God's Word. It cannot be moved. Sometimes, we might feel like we are on shaky ground, but we are not. Put your hope in God. As one man once wrote: "There are two graces which Christ uses above all to fill the soul with joy: faith and hope. Faith tells the soul what Christ has done for it and so comforts it; hope revives the soul with the news of what Christ will do: both draw at one tap—Christ and his promises." Growing in the stillness of the Lord reminds us that we have these two graces: faith and hope. With the rope of God's sure faithfulness and the anchor of his hope, we stand firm in Christ's promises, not afraid that we will drift into the currents of despair or hopelessness. This is our confidence:

> *If on earth my days he lengthen,*
> *He my weary soul will strengthen;*
> *All my trust in him I place.*
> *Earthly wealth is not abiding,*
> *Like a stream away is gliding;*
> *Safe I anchor in his grace. (CW 421)*

DAY 14:

Our Journey

Friday, February 27, 2004

Morning of 2/27
Dear Friends in Christ,

I think this e-mail will be relatively short. Yesterday started out good, but then we had a minor setback. The sensor that was used to measure Kris's brain pressure had apparently shifted. When they came to readjust it to the proper place, it showed that her brain pressure was a little higher than what it had been reading. For this reason, they put Kris back on the paralyzing medicine. The doctor said we took three steps forward and one step back. What are we going to look at: the one step back or the three steps forward? Our nature with all its failures, sins and weakness would naturally look at the one step back, but our Lord encourages us and reminds us to look at the three steps forward. My simple mind puts it into this illustration: what happens when your car gets stuck in the snow? You go back and forth until you pop out. Well, I think we are just in one of those backup modes until we start moving forward. The doctor stated that we may have several of these "backup times" before we finally pop out. So, what are we to do? As the psalmist says: "We wait upon the Lord." As you enter your weekend, enjoy God's blessings that are around you, remember to pray and remember to celebrate the Lord's Day. Remaining in Him, Mark and Kris

Afternoon of 2/27
Dear Friends in Christ,

I know that some of you already received an e-mail, but some things changed before I got the update out to everyone, so here is a new update. First of all, welcome to those who are joining us just recently on our e-mail connection. I am reminded of what our Lord says in Galatians 6:2: "Carry each other's burdens, and in this way you will fulfill the law of Christ." Elsewhere, God reminds us that the fulfillment of the law is love. While resting my eyes on the green couch this morning (by the way, I will never, ever buy a green couch), I had a dream that I was sitting in the waiting room and all these people were standing behind me. Some I knew and some I didn't. This is what this passage says to me, and I appreciate all those who have told me that these updates make them feel like they are here with us and praying with us. Thank you for carrying our burdens with us. Concerning Kris, it seems like the low brain pressure numbers were not quite accurate. This morning the doctor put in a new sensor, and the numbers are now a little higher. In addition, he is recommending that we put in a trachea tube so that the ventilator can go into that tube so as to give her airway and mouth some relief, also, a feeding tube. It appears she may be on the ventilator for at least another week. The surgeon came in (our good one from the last two surgeries) and said he wanted to wait until Monday to do this so as to give Kris some time to bring the numbers down. So here we continue our roller coaster ride. This morning was another difficult moment, but it is amazing how God's Word comforts us with the thought: "Be still, and know that I am God." I once again ask that you help carry this burden to our Lord and seek that he swoop down from the heavens and touch her head with his healing finger. We are reminded not to look at the one step we have taken back, but to look at the several steps we have taken forward. The sun is out shining today, and Kris and I both pray for all of you that your weekend is full of God's goodness, mercy and the sweet meditation on his word.

God's blessings to you. Mark and Kris

DAY 14:

Your Journey

**"But those who hope in the Lord will renew their strength.
They will soar on wings like eagles; they will run and
not grow weary, they will walk and not be faint."**
ISAIAH 40:31

N o discussion of hope would be complete if we did not turn to this great chapter of Isaiah. Having hope in the stillness of the Lord means that we are strengthened by the Lord.

Really? I will run? But cancer has sapped my strength and I need help getting out of bed. I will walk? Really? A stroke has crippled me so that I stagger from bed to chair.

Oh, that we would have the faith of beautiful Ethel. Living to months short of her 100th birthday, she was a godly example of one whose spirit was renewed even as her body was succumbing to the ravages of old age and illness. "Pastor," she expressed with confidence, "for me it is not one day at a time. No, it is one moment at a time, for Jesus is with me. I lift up my eyes to Jesus and he renews me."

These words from Isaiah are very closely connected to the words of Psalm 91: "He who dwells in the shelter of the Most High will rest in the shadow of the Almighty. I will say of the Lord, 'He is my refuge and my fortress, my God, in whom I trust. Surely he will save you from the fowler's snare and from the deadly pestilence. He will cover you with his feathers, and under his wings you will find refuge.'" What a privilege to share those words of Psalm 91 and Isaiah 40 with Ethel and see her faith shine in the midst of declining health.

The same is true of Lord Craven, who lived in London at the time of the bubonic plague. He resolved to move to his country home. While getting ready, he overheard one of his servants say, "I suppose my master is leaving London to avoid the plague as if his God lives in the country and not in the town." In response, Lord Craven expressed, "My God lives everywhere and can preserve me in town as well as in the country. I will stay where I am. The ignorance of my servant has just now preached to me a very useful sermon. Lord, pardon this unbelief and the distrust of your care which made me think of running from your hand." Lord Craven stayed in London, was very useful to his sick neighbors and never caught the plague.

Wherever we are, whatever the circumstance of life, our hope is in the Lord, for he is our strong deliverer. With the hymnist, we find great confidence in our Lord:

If you but trust in God to guide you And place your confidence in him,
He'll give you strength and stand beside you When days are dreary, dark, and dim.
For those who trust his changeless love Build on the rock that does not move.

(CW 444)

Week 3
Be Still in the Midst of Family Need

The devotions for "Your Journey" will lead us from Jesus' words from the cross, "Behold your son…. Behold your mother" to encourage us to Be Still in times of family difficulties.

DAY 15:

Our Journey

Saturday, February 28, 2004

Good Morning from Theda Clark! What a beautiful morning here in the heart of the Fox Valley, with the sun shining off the river next to the hospital! Where else would one want to be on a beautiful sunny morning in February in Wisconsin? I remember that today I was scheduled for part of the polar plunge in Tomahawk. I was looking forward to that. I had my congregational evangelist convinced that we would do it together dressed up as identical Siamese twins. But that will be another year. Our journey continues with more of the same. Kris had a good night, and her numbers continue to be below 20. We, however, need to see her numbers consistently below 10 before we can begin to think about waking her up. She will be heading to CAT scan and then wait for the doctor's arrival. For some reason, the swelling in her brain just doesn't want to come down. The doctor said that this happens with young brains. Just wait until I can tell her that the doctor called her young. A younger brain is more sensitive and thus more susceptible to swelling. So take heart, all those who are around Kris's age—you are young not only at heart, but young in brain. Last night, several family and friends joined me for my nightly devotion with Kris. I read Psalm 86 as if Kris were reading it. I often would change a word to reflect Kris's situation. For example, David says, "a band of ruthless men seeks my life." So I read to Kris this as we prayed: "Cancer is attacking me, O God, a tumor and swelling seeks my life, but you, O Lord, are a compassionate and gracious God, slow to anger, abounding in love and faithfulness. Turn to me and have mercy on me; grant your strength to your servant. Give me a sign of your goodness ... for you, O Lord, have helped me and comforted me." As you pray today, insert what your trial and problem is, and know that the Lord continues to hear. Also, pray for the others here. We have several new families added to our CCU waiting room. A mother collapsed with a brain bleed, and her daughter's wedding is today. A man was in for a routine laser surgery, and the laser missed and hit his bladder. Others as well. So, it is a privilege to sit with these people, and how quickly they seek comfort and assurance from the Lord. Actually, I am becoming the "old-timer" here, and so they often say, "Ask Mark, he probably knows." People often ask me what they can do. When I think of it, the best things you can do for us is first of all, pray. Then, take care of yourself, especially in your spiritual life. Take time for the Lord and let him fill your heart with all of his Word and promises. I get this from Kris, who taught me so often by her words and attitude to think of others first. She does that so well.

God's Blessings to you this weekend.

From our CCU hearts to yours, have a great day and a super Lord's Day.

Mark and Kris

DAY 15:

Your Journey

"Here is your son…. Here is your mother."
JOHN 19:26-27

As we once more look up to the cross, we hear our Lord speak for the third time. In his words of love and care for his mother, we can be encouraged to be still in the midst of family need. We can make many plans, we have many goals in life, but it all comes to a halt in the face of family need. When our loved ones are suffering, so do we, and nothing seems to matter except to help them.

In the midst of his suffering, Job confesses that it is God who made him: "Your hands shaped me and made me…. Remember that you molded me like clay…. Did you not pour me out like milk and curdle me like cheese [this figurative language refers to development in the womb], clothe me with skin and flesh and knit me together with bones and sinews? You gave me life and showed me kindness and in your providence watched over my spirit." Some may choose to believe that this marvelous body just evolved over millions of years. With Job, we know that it is our God who made us in a unique way and gave us both body and soul. Our Lord sustains both the body and soul. Throughout our lives, he has shown kindness, extending way back to the day Jesus climbed the cross for our salvation, and all those gifts became ours the day we were baptized. Rejoice today that all of us are wondrously made and God's gift of salvation extends to us all. Believe in this, and you can look fear in the face and gain strength and courage.

What sorrow must have filled the heart of Mary as she looked up at her son on the cross. Although she knew that he needed to do this, yet it was a "sword that pierced her heart." Suffering for the sins of the whole world, Jesus did not overlook the needs of his own family—his mother. In his gracious love, he provided for her even in his dying hours. After the Lord provided Abraham with a ram to sacrifice in place of his son Isaac, "Abraham called the place The Lord will provide. And to this day it is said, 'On the mount of the LORD it shall be provided.'" On the mount of the Lord—Mount Calvary—our Lord provided for his mother and her need. On that same mount, our Lord looks down from the cross on our family and our need and provides for us. These thoughts led the preacher John Newton to pen these words:

Though troubles assail us and dangers affright
Though friends should all fail us and foes all unite
Yet one things secures us, whatever betide,
The promise assures us, "The Lord will provide."

("Though Troubles Assail Us" from Songbook: Then Sings My Soul)

DAY 16:

Our Journey

Sunday, February 29, 2004

Dear Friends in Christ,

"I was glad when they said to me, 'Let us go to the house of the Lord.'" In a few moments, I am going to get ready for worship. What a wonderful blessing to get up on a Sunday morning and be focused on spending a few moments in the Lord's house. I cherish those moments. This morning, as I worship, I have more people added to my prayer list. I have all my new "comrades in arms"—those other families facing their battles in the CCU. In addition, I pray for all of you. Right now, I just paused to pray that God would bless you today and that you would have your place of worship in God's house. Kris is again doing well. Remember the analogy that I have used of rocking your car back and forth to get out of the mud? It seems we are rocking forward today. Could this be the time that we pop out, or will we have to rock back once again? Only God knows. But if all goes as is now, once again the doctor will be thinking of taking her off the paralyzing drug, which is one more step forward. Tomorrow, however, Kris will have a trach tube put in, as well as a feeding tube. In the context of all that we are dealing with, these are good things, as they will help Kris when she wakes up.

Lord's Day blessings from Theda Clark CCU.
Mark and Kris

DAY 16:

Your Journey

"The Lord is my shepherd, I shall not be in want."
PSALM 23:1

When I was younger, I learned this psalm in the King James translation which read: "The Lord is my shepherd, I shall not want." It took me a long time to understand this verse, for I was wondering: "Why wouldn't I want him if he is my shepherd?" Then, some kind person helped me realize what the words meant. With Jesus as my Good Shepherd, I will not want for anything.

Really? I shall not want for anything—I shall not be in want? This is hard to understand when the needs of our family arise. Sitting down to pay the bills, the check doesn't cover the cost. Our children need clothes for school, money for tuition. Our car is breaking down and we need better transportation. Our children need braces. One of our loved ones is sick and the hospital bills are mounting. The list goes on.

This week in our meditation on the stillness of our Lord, we are reminded that our Lord does care for our physical needs. As we seek Jesus' third word from the cross, we are reminded how our Lord took care of his mother. In the last hours of life, he did not forget her, but provided for her physical welfare. In Jesus' world, widows had a very difficult lot in life. Most women depended on their husbands for their earthly support. If their husband died, widows were dependent on any adult children or were often were reduced to a life of begging. For Mary, Jesus would not be there to help her. But, he provided for her. His disciple, John, would take care of her.

The shepherd always provides for the sheep. Our Good Shepherd always provides for our needs even in the face of our greatest need. Sheep trust their shepherd. We trust Jesus and continue to walk in the stillness of the Lord as we are comforted once again:

Be still, my soul; The Lord is on your side;
Bear patiently, in midst of family need
We give you thanks for family so dear
In agony you lovingly proclaimed
"My dear friend John, behold your new mother
My grieving mother, here behold your son."

(Modified verse from CW 415)

DAY 17:

Our Journey

Monday, March 1, 2004

Dear Friends in Christ,

Good morning as we begin a new week here at Theda Clark. All last week, while the sun was shining, we were uncertain about Kris's condition. But today it is gloomy out, and the rain is filtering down to wash away the messy residue left behind from recent snowstorms. During a conversation with a friend, we remarked how it is during the crucible of suffering that many layers are stripped away. The layers of possessions, hobbies, goals and plans are all stripped away and what is left is our relationship with our Savior, Jesus. Since this is what is most important and what we cling to during sufferings and trials, wouldn't we want to strengthen that relationship before our suffering? But God has a way of teaching us lessons. It is now Day 19, and God has taught us some valuable lessons about the steadfastness of his love and mercy. He renews us once again today. He renews us with his love and presence, but he has also renewed us in a special way today—get ready for this—Kris opened her eyes today and is beginning to wake up. Yesterday, we took off her paralyzing drugs and sedation, and she responds to our names. For the first time in over 16 days, we have seen those wonderful eyes shining out to us, and there has been an ever so slight squeezing of the hand. "Praise the Lord, all you nations, extol him all you peoples, for great is his love toward us, and the faithfulness of the Lord endures forever." We realize that we still have many mountains to climb and valleys to traverse, but we will take the joy of this moment. There may also be a temporary setback today, as they probably will put the trach tube in this afternoon, which means she will undergo minor surgery. But, the joy of the moment remains, and I just had to share that joy with you who have walked in prayer with me for these past 19 days. The nurse was commenting that the standard rule of thumb is four days of recovery for every one day like this, so we know that the journey is still before us, but God renews us each day. Kris and I both send our love and blessings and thankfulness for all your love and support. God's Blessings, and as we begin another week let us sing like the hymnist: "With the Lord begin thy task, Jesus will direct it." Mark and Kris

DAY 17:

Your Journey

"Jesus was in the stern, sleeping."
MARK 4:38

An unchurched man once accused a pastor: "All you talk about is heaven, angels and glories to come. I'm interested in things that are now. You speak about spiritual things, forgiveness, peace. My concern is getting enough food for my children to eat. Christ—all you talk about is Christ! He wants to give me salvation. He wants to give me heaven, you say. Give me someone who is practical and something that is for today."

This man spoke from a heart focused on the things of this world – a heart that didn't have the slightest idea of what Christianity really is. When he says that Christianity has nothing to do with today and that Jesus isn't practical, he is all wrong.

It is true that our emphasis on living in the stillness has centered mainly on the spiritual affairs of our lives. It should, because our soul is a million times more important than our body.

The story before us, though, in which Jesus calms the sea, reminds us that our Savior loves us entirely—both body and soul.

While Jesus and his disciples were traveling across the Sea of Galilee, a sudden storm—common on that body of water—descended on the boat. Frantically, the disciples struggled to keep the boat afloat, but it was in danger of being swamped. But where was Jesus? Sleeping in the stern. Sleeping? How could Jesus sleep while the boat was tossed back and forth by the storm? Here we have the perfect example of the stillness of the Lord, demonstrated by the Lord himself—the author of stillness. Even though sleeping, he was still in control, and nothing would happen without his consent. The disciples exhibited a measure of hopelessness as they asked, "Don't you care if we drown?" They went to the right person—that was good. But they went to him with the wrong attitude.

Have you seen the devastation caused by a tornado? Strong buildings are reduced to rubble. A lifetime of work is decimated in minutes. For all our strength, the forces of nature are too much for us. It may seem that way when family needs arise. Try as hard as we might, we cannot stop disease and sickness, financial woe and personal conflict or that last great obstacle: death. On our journey, we walk through many valleys. But, we walk not alone. Our hearts may wonder if Jesus is "sleeping" while we are struggling, but let us be reminded that there is no storm that is out of the control of our Savior as the hymnist sings:

> *Yea, though I walk through death's dark vale,*
> *Yet will I fear no ill; For thou are with me, and thy rod*
> *And staff me comfort still. (CW 360)*

DAY 18:

Our Journey

Tuesday, March 2, 2004

Dear Friends in Christ,

Good morning from Theda Clark's CCU. Our Lord always reminds us that those who wait on the Lord, who lean on his promises, will always be renewed in spirit. We have been continued to be renewed by the Lord's awesome working in our lives. Kris made good progress yesterday. She opens her eyes wide, follows me with her eyes, and reacts to the sound of our voices, and last night before I went to bed, she slightly squeezed my hand when I asked her. The breathing machine is set at 8 breaths per minute, and she is consistently at 15-16, which means half are on her own. We did not do the trach yesterday, they wanted to give her another 24 hours, and it is a 50/50 chance that they may not. I can tell she may be getting some of her spunk back because I told her that I was going to get something to eat with my brother and she slightly shook her head no. She also tried to talk. But, I told her that right now she can't talk and for now she has to sit and listen to me. I had better get all my words in now. I sat by her bed last night and finally fell asleep and the nurse sent me off. I think Kris was up quite a bit because she seems sleepy this morning. "Praise the Lord, O my soul, and forget not all his benefits." Yes, we praise the Lord for his goodness and praise him for your support. Our battle will continue to be long, but we clearly see our Savior, Jesus, right out in front of us. Continue to pray and continue to fight. God's Blessings, Mark

DAY 18:

Your Journey

"The disciples woke him and said to him,
'Teacher, don't you care if we drown?'"
MARK 4:38

"Don't you care if we drown?" The disciples came to their sleeping Lord. How often don't similar questions come out of our mouths? "Don't you care that my wife has cancer?" "Don't you care that my child is sick?" "Don't you care that I can't pay the bills?" "Don't you care that I'm unhappy in this marriage?" "Don't you care that I find no satisfaction in my work?" "Don't you care that I have no friends?" Don't you care...? Don't you care? Does the Lord really care?

Let's take a stroll back to the Garden of Eden. As Satan tempted Eve, he drove a wedge of doubt about God's care. "You will not surely die,... for God knows that when you eat of it,... you will be like God, knowing good and evil." In other words, God just wants to keep you down. He doesn't really care about you. He just wants to take all the fun out of life and fill your life with hardship and toil and struggle. Those same words—different situations, but the same words—are used to tempt us also.

Is God to blame for all of our heartache and suffering? There is nothing bad, evil or sorrowful that is the Lord's fault. God did not create cancer. He does not cause financial stress or tension in marriages. These are all a result of sin. Some of our problems are a result of sin in general—that is, we simply live in a sinful world that is decaying. Many diseases come from the fact that our bodies are not perfect. However, other problems are a result of a specific sin that we have committed.

Living in the stillness of the Lord means that instead of focusing on our problems, our eyes are focused on the Lord, our Savior. There was another incident that took place on the water. At another time, when the disciples were struggling in a storm, Jesus came to them walking on the water. After being invited by Jesus, Peter also stepped out on the water and began to walk. As long as he kept his eyes focused on the Savior, he kept walking. But then he did a very human thing—he looked down! He looked down at the waves. Wow—they were big! He looked at the wind—the weather was wicked! He looked at the water—it was deep! If he had kept his eyes focused on the Lord, he would not have considered the wicked weather, the huge waves or the deep, dark water. But he looked down, and with that, the stillness of the Lord left his heart—and he sank.

My dear grandmother had a picture of this scene in her bedroom. I have since inherited the picture. My grandmother's life did not begin well, as her mother died when she was young. Having a child out of wedlock, my grandmother never married. She raised her child on her own. My grandmother was not perfect, and she endured many storms. Knowing what I know about my grandmother, that picture was symbolic of her life. In each and every storm, she called out to the Lord and the Lord was there. You see, I left out one detail about the incident with Peter. As he was sinking, Peter cried out, "Lord, help." The Lord grabbed Peter, and they got back into the boat. And the Bible says, "It was still." When we are sinking beneath the waves of doubt, the Lord lifts us up, and when we look into his face, it is still.

The Lord's my shepherd, I'll not want. He makes me down to lie
In pastures green; He leadeth me The quiet waters by. (CW 360)

DAY 19:

Our Journey

Thursday, March 4, 2004

Dear Friends in Christ,

Remember the Hallelujah Chorus in Handel's Messiah? That has been ringing from the soon-to-be-vacated CCU room 107!! I cried unto the Lord, "O Lord, Hear my cry for mercy," and he has answered ... as we knew he would! Kris is awake, talking non-stop, and wanting to eat. These are the doctor's own words: "This is miraculous." The nurses are all coming in and saying that they have never seen someone come out so quickly after being out for so long. As I relate to her all that has happened, she just says, "Wow—I can't believe this happened to me." She even has her spunk back, as she called our daughters on the phone this morning for the first time. To Kayla she said, "When I get out of here, we are going to Disney." Hallelujah! So much has happened in the last 24 hours—the breathing tube taken out, sensors taken out of her head, conversations and questions with her, passing one test after another. Actually, last night, toward the end, I was wishing for company because all Kris wanted to do is talk and I was running out of things to tell her. But it was a great time to slowly fill her in on all the details. This morning she was awake at 6 and ready to go. After her swallow study she will be transferred up to 2nd floor. Hallelujah! After spending over 22 days down here, there is both joy and a moment of sadness because I am leaving behind some families who are still in CCU. One family last evening had just had to intubate their loved one, and the look in their eyes was the same look I felt on February 14. I sat with them for a while in the CCU waiting room and prayed for them. What is sad is they have left the church and so their foundation is so shaky. My other dear friends that I met have to make the decision of taking their mother off of life-support. We go up to the second floor to join our friends that left before us and leave behind others. What an experience these past 22 days have been! As we go up to second floor, I know some are asking about visiting. Let me just share this: we appreciate all those who have and will stop to visit. However, as with Kris's last surgery, I am going to be very protective about the amount and length of visitors. We have no problem with people coming, but I advise that your visit would be of a short duration. I have been personally strengthened by those many friends who have just stopped by for a brief visit. Short and more frequent visits are much better. Also, I am not sure about these regular updates. I may not be able to get down here every day. But we will write as often as we can. Our journey is by no means over, but as Kris says to say to you: "Tell them there is light at the end of the tunnel. Thank you all." You have walked with me to heaven's door and carried the load, now let us go to heaven's door and greet the Savior with our loud Hallelujahs. Yesterday, two doctors were in the room at the same time, and we were high-fiving each other. Right now, high-five someone for me—and then, all together—let's hear it—Hallelujah! Hallelujah! Hallelujah! Hallelujah! Hallelujah! Mark and Kris

DAY 19:

Your Journey

"Cast all your anxiety on him for he cares for you."
1 PETER 5:7

I n his book *Lectures to my Students,* famous preacher Charles Spurgeon warns about the dangers of depression and discouragement in the public ministry: "Fits of depression come over most of us…. The strong are not always vigorous, the wise not always ready, the brave not always courageous, and the joyous not always happy."

Pastors are not immune to the temptations of discouragement. The greatest example of this is the prophet, Elijah. Having just accomplished a great victory over the prophets of the false god, Baal, and with many people turning back to faith in the true God, Elijah suddenly became depressed and ran away. Frank Graeff, a lively and exuberant Methodist preacher around the turn of the 20th century, faced his own struggle with depression after suffering from a series of heartaches. As joyful as he had once been, so great now was his darkness and sorrow. In the midst of that painful experience, he wrote the words of the hymn "Does Jesus care?"

> *Does Jesus care when my heart is pained Too deeply for mirth or song,*
> *As the burdens press, and the cares distress, And the way grows weary and long?*

> *Does Jesus care when my way is dark With a nameless dread and fear?*
> *As the daylight fades into deep night shades, Does he care enough to be near?*

Does Jesus care when I've tried and failed To resist some temptation strong;
When for my deep grief I find no relief, Though my tears flow all the night long?

Does Jesus care when I've said "goodbye" To the dearest on earth to me,
And my sad heart aches till it nearly breaks—Is it aught to Him? Does he see?

The thing about this hymn is that each verse has a refrain to it. This hymn was really inspired by today's verse from 1 Peter, which encourages us to cast our cares on our God. In other words, we are to commit our burdens to the Lord. Philippians 4 reminds us not to be anxious about anything, but to come to the Lord in prayer. Spend time in the Word, and you will find a promise for every one of your needs. Does he care? Yes—we know the answer to be yes. How do we know? Take a look at the cross, and you see that he cares, as Graeff expressed in his hymn's refrain:

Oh, yes, He cares, I know He cares, His heart is touched with my grief;
When the days are weary, the long nights dreary, I know my Savior cares.

("Does Jesus Care?" from Songbook: Then Sings My Soul)

DAY 20:

Our Journey

Saturday, March 6, 2004

Dear Friends in Christ,

Psalm 107 says, "Give thanks to the Lord, for he is good; his love endures forever. Let the redeemed of the Lord say this....Whoever is wise, let him heed these things and consider the great love of the Lord." Throughout the psalm, the writer speaks of people in different situations and trials. Through it all, we can count on one thing: the love of the Lord. God has shown his mercy toward us not just because of the physical recovery but more importantly because we have been redeemed. Those last words say—if you are wise, you will listen to these things. We pray that you may be wise this Lenten season and listen to the love of the Lord as seen in his Passion for us. We also are so grateful for the many expressions of love and support. I just left Kris at our soon-to-be vacated room on the second floor. Yes—as the song goes—we are moving on up to the 6th floor—rehabilitation floor. All tubes and such are out except for one IV, which will soon be gone. Kris said to say that "All is going well and we are thankful for all." She continues to make progress every day with the return of her humor and spunk. Movement continues to come back to her body. This morning for the first time she lifted her right hand to her mouth. She is moving her legs. She cannot sit up herself, much less walk. But more and more she is moving her body around herself. At this time, part of her throat muscles are still weak, so she is on thickened liquids. But she still keeps asking for water and Luigi's pizza. She has us laughing all day with her comments and quick wit. More and more hospital workers keep popping in because they have to see this "miracle." The doctor said to her yesterday that if she were a cat she would have used up several of her lives already. She keeps inviting everyone to her brother-in-law's retirement party. He will have to go back to work to pay for this party. Also, she keeps planning a trip to Disney in Florida.

Now for rehab. We can expect one to two weeks of rehab before returning home. However, I am still taking one day at a time. There may be plateaus or setbacks, but the Lord has taught us to cherish the moment and deal with the next one when it comes. Her room number will be 675—on the water side!—and her days will be full of rehab. Visitation is best after 4:00, with short visits a good thing. We don't mind visitors, but please keep this in mind.

Tomorrow is the Lord's Day, and as the psalmist says: "Whoever is wise, let him heed these things"—whoever is wise will be hearing God's Word in God's House. Kris's prayer last night was to soon go home and go back to church. Amen—may it be soon. God's Blessings, Mark and Kris

DAY 20:

Your Journey

"He got up, rebuked the wind and said to the waves, 'Quiet! Be still!'"
MARK 4:39

During seminary, I wrote my first-ever sermon on this portion of God's word, and as I tried to come up with an imaginative theme, my mind turned to the 1980s hit movie *Ghostbusters*, in which three off-the-edge professors get rid of the ghosts that haunt people's lives. The movie's tagline was "Who ya gonna call? Ghostbusters!" So, I thought I'd tweak it a bit to apply to God: "Who ya gonna call? Stormbuster!" I eventually decided that the theme was just a little *too* imaginative, but the parallel remains. When we need a storm busted in our lives, who are we going to call?

For the past several days, we have watched the disciples in the boat. They needed a storm busted—literally—and they turned to the Lord. Despite the fact that they did so with doubt and apprehension, the Lord answered their prayer. All Jesus had to do was speak, and the storm dissipated. Wouldn't it have been astounding to be on the boat that day? One minute, you are struggling for life, and the next minute, the waters are placid and smooth. One minute, your heart is filled with anxiety and fear, and the next, you are standing in awe of the stillness of the Lord.

In one artist's rendition of this event, Jesus stands in the boat, commanding the wind and waves to stop. But with him are not the 12 disciples; instead, the boat is filled with people from all walks of life. People like you and me. Look at the waves that Jesus is about to command to be still. What waves are rocking your boat? Is it disease or illness? Are the effects of old age or a youthful injury affecting you? Do tensions rise in your marriage or with your children? Do matters of finance weigh heavily upon you? Is your job threatened, or are there conflicts with co-workers? Are you enduring a special temptation—a temptation to lie or to commit adultery or to steal? Stand at that picture and place your problems in place of the waves. As you do so, hear the Lord calm you with his stillness—hear him say to you: "Be still _____ (insert problem)." And then wait as you see the Lord calming your heart and mind with his love.

After the death of this young wife, Elisha Hoffman returned to his home in Pennsylvania and devoted the next 33 years of his life to pastoring Benton Harbor Presbyterian Church. One day, while making calls on the sick, he met a woman who seemed to have incurable depression. She opened up her heart to him and poured out her many sorrows. Wringing her hands, she said, "What shall I do? What shall I do?" The griefs that Pastor Hoffman had faced in life had prepared him for this moment. He knew that the only comfort was in the Lord. He said to the woman, "You cannot do better than to take all your sorrows to Jesus. You must tell Jesus." Suddenly, the lady's face lit up. "Yes!" she cried out. "That's it! I must tell Jesus." Her words echoed in his ears and led his heart to write this hymn:

> *I must tell Jesus All of my trials, I cannot bear these burdens alone;*
> *In my distress He kindly will help me, He ever loves and cares for his own.*

> *I must tell Jesus! I must tell Jesus! I cannot bear my burdens alone;*
> *I must tell Jesus! I must tell Jesus! Jesus can help me, Jesus alone.*
>> *("I Must Tell Jesus" from Songbook: Then Sings My Soul)*

DAY 21:

Our Journey

Monday, March 8, 2004

Dear Friends in Christ,

Good Morning from Theda Clark! Right now it is 3 a.m., but don't be alarmed. Kris and I are just sitting here in the computer room on 6th floor out for our usual 3 a.m. stroll. That's right; Kris is up sitting in a wheelchair next to me. The weekend brought wonderful progress for Kris. On Saturday, when we moved to the rehab floor, Kris could not sit up on her own or sit in place on her own. Yesterday, with assistance, she sat up and now sits in place on her own. She has even stood in place with assistance several times! Although she says that her hands and legs feel heavy, she continues to move them more and more each day. I now live in the room with Kris and tomorrow—or later today—we begin our intensive therapy of three hours a day. On Saturday morning, one of my good pastor friends shared with me a devotion on Moses' song of praise after walking through the Red Sea. With Moses, we sing: "I will sing to the Lord for he is highly exalted.... The Lord is my strength and my song; he has become my salvation. He is my God, and I will praise him." Remember the account of crossing the Red Sea. The Israelites were trapped with the Sea on one side and the Egyptian army on the other. But God stood as a pillar of fire to protect them from the Egyptians while he parted the sea for his people to walk through. Even though the Israelites grumbled against God and did not trust, He still delivered them. We felt trapped with death on one side and the inability to control the swelling on the other. But the Lord parted the way for this recovery. We maybe did not see the way at the time, but the Lord knew the path to deliverance. That path comes to us straight through the cross of our dear Savior. Last night, with a number of us around

Kris, we sang the doxology—"Praise God from whom all blessings flow. Praise him all creature here below. Praise him above ye heavenly host. Praise Father, Son and Holy Ghost." Although this is not an experience I would wish on anyone, since we had to go through it, I thank my Lord for the opportunities to witness. Monday evening I will be attending the funeral of a lady who was in CCU with Kris. I got to know the family very well and shared the Word with them. Right before they took her off of the respirator, they invited me in to share the Word and prayer with them. I have no idea what God did with the Word I shared or if it reached her ears. But all this is worth the experience if some were strengthened in their faith and someday we will see them in heaven. Well, I better wrap this up. As I shuffle Kris off to bed, she would like say, "Thank you for all the prayers, care and concern. I keep fighting the road ahead. I miss you all very much and hope to see you soon. I miss listening to WJJQ with Mark in the Morning." The doctor was in and again he said, "This is a miracle, Kris, you were almost dead." He also said that the rehab would be long and tough but that it all goes to attitude. Most people in this situation he said will go through a period of depression as well as other stages. He encouraged her not to get down but to keep looking at her goals. Kris has a great attitude and a great goal. Her goal is not only to get to "Luigi's pizza" but more importantly to "get home and back to church." From our rehab hearts to yours,

God's Blessings,
Mark and Kris

DAY 21:

Your Journey

"Give us today our daily bread."
MATTHEW 6:11

In the Fourth Petition of the Lord's Prayer, we are instructed to pray for what we need "this day." Later in Matthew 6, Jesus say, "Do not worry about tomorrow, for tomorrow will worry about itself. Each day has enough trouble of its own." How often we are tempted to look ahead to the next day. Living in the stillness of the Lord means we do not look to tomorrow with fear and worry. Rather, we live today in thankfulness for what we have.

As I have served God's people for the past 23 years, I have had the privilege to become friends with some awesome children of God. One of the ladies who will always stand out as a cherished friend is Ethel Nyberg. At 99 years of age, Ethel endured many trials and challenges in life. Yet, a more cheerful and godly lady I have not met. I once mentioned to her that we just take one day at a time. "Oh no, Pastor," she responded, "for me—I take one hour at a time." May we all have the same attitude of trust and confidence as dear Ethel, who now lives forever with her Lord.

Karolina Sandell, daughter of Swedish pastor Jonas Sandell, also knew what it was like to live day by day. Though frail in body, she had a strong spirit, feasting on the artistic, literary and religious influences of her home life. But tragedy struck when she was 26. She and her father were enjoying a boat trip on the east coast of Sweden when suddenly the ship lurched. Before her eyes, her father was pitched overboard and drowned. Returning home alone, Karolina began using Scripture to process her grief. In the hymn "Day by Day," she gives us insight into her personal experience with the daily strength the Lord provides for His struggling children:

Day by day, and with each passing moment,
Strength I find, to meet my trials here;
Trusting in my father's wise bestowment,
I've no cause for worry or fear.
He whose heart is kind beyond all measure
Gives unto each day what he deems best—
Lovingly, its part of pain and pleasure,
Mingling toil with peace and rest.

Every day, the Lord Himself is near me
With a special mercy for each hour;
All my cares He fain would bear, and cheer me,
He whose name is Counselor and Power.
The protection of his child and treasure
Is a charge that on Himself He laid;
"As thy days, thy strength shall be in measure,"
This the pledge to me He made.
                    ("Day by Day" from Songbook: Then Sings My Soul)

Week 4

Be Still in the Midst of Loneliness

The devotions for "Your Journey" will lead us from Jesus' words from the cross, "My God, my God, why have you forsaken me?" to encourage us to Be Still even when we feel alone.

DAY 22:

Our Journey

Tuesday, March 9, 2004

Dear Friends in Christ,

Good Morning from Theda Clark. When was the last time you took a drink of water? How easy it is. As we continue our rehab, Kris continues to make progress. However, she is still on thickened liquids, which means she cannot drink water. Every day, we drink water, and sometimes we spill or waste it—but we certainly take it for granted. One of Kris's goals is to soon drink a cup of water. She is thirsty for this. But I will tell you one thing she is not thirsty for—the water of life. Yes, she desires the water of life, but the Lord has filled her in abundance with this refreshing water that comes through Jesus by his Word. That water of life is sitting right in our homes in those wonderful words of life our Lord has given us. It is this word that has sustained us and will continue to lift our hearts in Jesus. These words and promises of Jesus help us in rehab. Kris often thinks she isn't doing well because she doesn't remember how far down she went. But, we are amazed by her progress. Yesterday, with much help, she took several halting, sliding but unmistakable steps. She still feels her limbs are very heavy and has a tough time with her fine motor skills. This morning, just as I was on my way to the pantry, a nurse walked in with a glass of thickened water. How wonderful for Kris. Today is a new day and we will begin this day with the Lord's water of life. Today, have a drink of water and thank the Lord for this simple act. This Lenten season, our prayer is that all of us would drink of the Living Water.

God's Blessings,
Mark and Kris

DAY 22:

Your Journey

"My God, my God, why have you forsaken me?"
MATTHEW 27:46

Alone—have you ever felt truly alone?

During some of the most difficult days while Kris was in the CCU, I felt more alone than I ever had in my life. It seemed that the doors of heaven had been closed to me. And I'm not the only one who has felt this way. Even our Lord experienced such a loneliness—such a "shutting of the door of heaven." On the cross, while suffering in the depths of hell, Jesus longed to look into the face of his heavenly Father, but he could not! There was no sweet vision of heaven. There was no Father to turn to. The doors of heaven had been shut tight. The Father turned his back on His Son and left him alone. Alone, Jesus was to struggle against Satan and to endure the agonies of hell.

Why? Why was the Father so against His Son? Look in the mirror, and you will see the answer. The Father turned from his Son because He loved you! It was all out of love for you that the Father sent his son to the cross, to bear your sins. Because Jesus bore our sins, our confidence is that the Father's face would always shine on us and the doors of heaven would be flung open to us.

Yes, we may very well be plagued with loneliness while on our earthly journey. Throughout this week, we will examine that loneliness. Yet, despite what we face, we will never be separated from our gracious God. The words of Romans 8 provide great encouragement: "For I am convinced that neither death nor life, neither angels nor demons, neither present nor the future, nor any powers, neither height nor depth nor anything else in all creation will be able to separate us from the love of God in Christ Jesus our Lord."

Notice the apostle says "us". Jesus didn't do this just for one or two or a select few. He did it for all, which means he did it for you!

With the great Lenten hymn, we lift our thanks to our Lord, who endured loneliness for our sakes:

> *Thou hast borne the smiting only*
> *That my wounds might all be whole;*
> *Thou hast suffered, sad and lonely,*
> *Rest to give my weary soul;*
> *Yea, the curse of God enduring,*
> *Blessing unto me securing.*
> *Thousand, thousand thanks shall be*
> *Dearest Jesus, unto thee. (CW 114)*

DAY 23:

Our Journey

Thursday, March 11, 2004

Dear Friends in Christ,

It is hard to believe, but four weeks ago today was when we began this journey. We entered the hospital anticipating a three- to four-day stay, and here we are. Throughout this journey, we have been sustained by the love of our Lord, as well as by your many expressions of love and support. To say "thank you" seems such a small thing compared to the huge appreciation that swells in our hearts for you. But right now we simply say this: We thank God often for you and your love and support. On Tuesday the doctors gathered for an assessment of Kris, and their thought is that she needs two to three weeks of therapy before discharge. However, she is making improvements every day and is now walking up and down the halls with a walker. We still suffer some bumps in the road from time to time and even experienced today some complications from the medicine but hope to get over these soon. By the end of the day, she is pretty wiped out from the intensive therapy. It is good that I can be with her to help her with her rest and also therapy. Today she will have a swallow study which will determine if she can get beyond thickened liquids. Pray that she passes and graduates to more solid food and possibly even to Luigi's. I just left her sleeping in her room. She is wiped out every night from the long day of therapy. The night provides a peaceful rest to recharge her batteries for the new day ahead. I pray that every night she has a peaceful rest to provide this time of recharging. Spiritually, we are recharged by the pastors who share God's Word with us and when we look into the Word and receive the peace that comes only through our Lord. Tonight, we watched a video of last week's Midweek Meditation in Tomahawk, and we were strengthened by the pastor's message. Like the disciples who slept while Jesus prayed in the Garden of Gethsemane, I too get weary. As Jesus said, "The Spirit is willing, but the flesh is weak." Yet, our God is good and grants peace at the end of the day and strength for the new day to come. My prayer is that all of us would have a peaceful night for physical recharging and a time of meditation around the Word for our spiritual recharging. From our 6th floor rehab hearts to yours,

God's Blessings.
Mark and Kris

DAY 23:

Your Journey

**"A time is coming, and has come, when you will
be scattered, each to his own home.
You will leave me all alone. Yet I am not
alone, for my Father is with me."**
JOHN 16:32

Webster's Dictionary defines loneliness as "being without company" or "cut off from others." The night before our Lord suffered on the cross, he predicted to his disciples that they would all leave him. First the multitudes in Galilee left him, and now his closest friends were about to flee also.

Psychiatrist Leonard Cammer has observed "The human being is the only species that can't survive alone. The human being needs another human being—otherwise he's dead! A telephone call to a depressed person can save a life. An occasional word, a ten-minute visit, can be more effective than twenty-four hours of nursing care. You can buy nursing care. You can't buy love."

According to his human nature, our Lord, too, desired human contact. Yet, those humans he had drawn closest to him—his friends—were now about to leave him. Why? As the forces of evil came to capture our dear Lord, his disciples—and even bold Peter—vanished into the darkness of the night out of fear. Our Lord was left alone to face those who unjustly accused him. No one stood up for him. No one came to his defense. As Isaiah prophesied, "Like one from whom men hide their faces he was despised, and we esteemed him not…. We all, like sheep, have gone astray, each of us has turned to his own way."

But Jesus was not alone. His Father stood beside him. Despite the lack of support from his friends, our Lord found comfort in the presence of the Heavenly Father. Even though he would some hours later cry out for his Father, in the Garden of Gethsemane, the Father's presence supplied the lack of all other company. Because God is our Father, he is with us, as He was with his own Son.

As we examine our loneliness throughout these next days we will be encouraged to remember that even when we don't feel God's presence in our lives, we know it because it is a fact.

Jesus, Thou are mine forever, Dearer far than earth to me;
Neither life nor death shall sever Those sweet ties which bind to Thee.

All were drear to me and lonely If thy presence gladdened not;
While I sing to Thee, Thee only, Mine's an ever blissful lot.

(The Lutheran Hymnal 357)

DAY 24:

Our Journey

Friday, March 12, 2004

Dear Friends in Christ,

Hello from 6th floor rehab at Theda Clark. Yesterday I was reminded of an old saying while trying to do my taxes: "Two things are certain: Death and Taxes." Well, that may be true, except there is one thing that is even more certain: "The Lord is my shepherd; I shall not want. He maketh to lie down in green pastures: He leadeth me beside the still waters. He restores my soul.... Yea, though I walk through the valley of the shadow of death, I will fear no evil: for thou art with me; Thy rod and thy staff they comfort me. Thou preparest a table before me in the presence of mine enemies: Thou anointest my head with oil; My cup runneth over. Surely goodness and mercy shall follow me all the days of my life: and I will dwell in the house of the Lord forever." This is even more certain than anything and is ours only through faith in Jesus. Jesus, the Good Shepherd, continues to uphold and comfort Kris. To compare: On Monday, she could not hold a pen or spoon in her hand. Yesterday, she fed herself for her lunch and wrote her name. On Monday, she could not sit on the edge of the bed without support; today, she walked around the halls of this half of the floor. On Monday, she could not grasp shirt or pants; today she dressed herself with "moderate" (as PT puts it) help. However, this week has not been without its bumps. Certain other problems have developed, though minor in nature, and still require further medical procedures. Also, the swallow study showed improvement in throat muscles but not enough for solid food. Yet, she did graduate to pureed foods, which Kris has enjoyed immensely. She fatigues very easily and requires much rest. Keep praying that some of these little "bumps" don't discourage but that she keeps strong in her spirit and attitude. She tries hard and gets frustrated because she wants to do more, which is good to a point. All in all, it has been a week of great progress. This morning, I heard some ripping sounds, and I turned and saw to my amazement that she was gripping a piece of mail, opening it and taking out the card. "The Lord is our shepherd" and continues to lead her to still waters and green pastures. Our prayer is that he lead you there this weekend as you gather together in worship around the words of our Good Shepherd.

God's Blessings.

Mark and Kris

DAY 24:

Your Journey

"My God, my God, why have you forsaken me?"
MATTHEW 27:46

I n one year, the average American today probably meets as many people as the average person did in a lifetime 100 years ago. And yet he's far lonelier. There's a big difference between being lonely and being alone, and the presence of other people doesn't necessarily matter. According to American psychiatrist and author Dr. Leonard Zunin, mankind's biggest problem is simply loneliness. In the dictionary of the 10 most impressive words, loneliness is described as the bitterest word.

There are few pains that go as deep as those caused by the feelings of loneliness—of being forsaken. Humans were created to be loved, and when love is withdrawn, the heart is deeply cut and hurt. A spanking might hurt a child but not nearly as much as the withdrawal of a parent's love. Youth can endure many hardships, but one thing that will get a young person down is the feeling that no one cares.

Loneliness was one of the worst pains Christ had to endure for our salvation. The priests, who should have been the first to welcome him, maligned and slandered him. The people of his hometown wanted to kill him. Even the disciples—who had seen his miracles—forsook him. Deeply as this must have hurt our Savior, he did not complain.

But now he has to face the worst kind of loneliness, as His father turns his face on him. From the cross, Jesus here quotes from Psalm 22: "My God, my God, why have you forsaken me? Why are you so far from saving me, so far from the words of my groaning?" As he looked toward the heavens, Jesus could not see his Father. In the midst of his deepest agony, he longed for a glimpse of his Father's loving face, but it was not there. In verse 3, the psalmist calls God the "Holy One." That is why Jesus was separated from the Father's loving face. God is holy—he hates sin. In Habakkuk 1:13, we read, "Your eyes are too pure to look on evil; you cannot tolerate wrong." God cannot and does not look on evil—so he could not and would not look on his son while our sins were upon him. In quoting Psalm 22, Jesus also knew the answer to his question. In effect, he was saying, "I understand Father. You are too holy, and I am full of sin—not mine, but the sins of others—you must give me this stroke from your divine wrath. But, Heavenly Father, this is the deepest pain of all—to not see your face."

It bears repeating. The reason Jesus was forsaken is that you and I have sinned. Christ was forsaken by God that we might never be. Thank God that because of what He did, we will never know eternal separation from our heavenly father. Today, take out your Bible and read through Psalm 22 in its entirety. Concentrate on each verse. Visualize the sights and sounds of Maundy Thursday and Good Friday, and watch as Psalm 22 adds special insight into these events. With verse 24, remember:

"For he has not despised or disdained the suffering of the afflicted one; he has not hidden his face from him but has listened to his cry for help."

DAY 25:

Our Journey

Sunday, March 14, 2004

Dear Brothers and Sisters of Redeemer,

Good Morning from 6th floor Theda Clark! As I was resting in my cot while Kris was eating her 3 a.m. Jell-o snack, I thought about the visits of some dear friends. Other than family, I have been keeping visitation down to a minimum in order to keep Kris rested for therapy. But looking back over the visits, I noticed how often we have spoken the words, "I love you." Why is it that we wait for times of testing and trial to speak such words? Kris and I truly can say and maybe haven't said it enough, "We love all of you at Redeemer. We thank God for you." But then I thought about how often I simply told God how much I love him. I thank, I praise, I admire him, stand in awe of him, and ask him for help—but to utter those words, "I love you, Lord." How often the Scriptures tell us that God loves us and shares his feelings for us both in words and actions. Today in your worship, I pray that you have had some personal time simply to share your love to your Lord and Savior. We love the Lord not simply because he has heard our prayer but because he has loved from before time and sent his Son to be our Savior. He who did not spare his own son for us but freely gave him up, now has also helped in our recent trial. Kris is doing well and continues to get stronger every day. Some side effects from the medicine are clearing up, and we are ready to begin a new week of therapy. She is walking more and more, and today the therapist will try some steps. Someone called last night and said they were sick of shoveling snow. I see none out my window. But I think both Kris and I would rather be shoveling snow with you in Tomahawk than sitting here—well, I better not say this too loud. God's Blessings on your worship today. I'm sure you have enjoyed Tom Park. Remember, he is a second-year student at Seminary, and our custom has been to have a door offering for him for the support of his services. Please be generous. This Wednesday, Pastor Kent Holz will be back filling in for me. Our days are very full of therapy, and by evening Kris is very tired. If I get time I may try to send another video greeting for worship this Wednesday. God willing, it will not be long and Kris and I will both be back. We will not try to wait until the snow melts.

God's Blessings, Mark and Kris

DAY 25:

Your Journey

> "Fear not, for I have redeemed you; I have
> summoned you by name; you are mine.
> When you pass through the waters, I will be with
> you; and when you pass through the rivers,
> they will not sweep over you."
> ISAIAH 43:1-2

"Loneliness, just plain loneliness is the most devastating disease," one doctor has said. "The longer I practice, the surer I am that there is no condition so acute, so universal. Everyone at one time or another is subject to its ravages. With many, the disease becomes chronic. And not a few live constantly under its blight—melancholy, bored, forlorn, friendless."

Have you experienced loneliness? For what reason? Have you moved to a new community far from your family? Has your mother or father, husband or wife been called home to heaven? Do you seem to be without good friends? Have your children moved? These and many other situations can stir up the feelings of loneliness. If you have experienced loneliness, you know the depth of these emotions. Sometimes we speak of places as being "God-forsaken." But for the Christian, no such place exists. In his book, John Eddison speaks of a small boy who had an atheistic father. He wanted his son to read aloud the words, "God is nowhere," but the boy got it wrong—or, rather, he got it right—he read, "God is now here."

"God is now here." These would be good words to repeat to ourselves. Better yet, add the words of God's stillness—"Be still, God is now here." Are you lonely because you are without loved ones? The Lord speaks to your soul: "Be still, God is now here, who has redeemed you." Do you feel forsaken because friends have left your side or you have been betrayed? The Lord speaks to your soul: "Be still, God is now here, who summons you by name." Do you feel despondent because your life is more full of problems and less full of friends? The Lord speaks to your soul: "Be still, God is now here, and you are mine."

The presence of our God can and does provide great comfort for us. Sometimes we call upon the Lord for help, but there is silence. It seems as though He is not even there. But He is there—He is there in His Word and Sacrament. The Lord is with us, close to us, as close as His Word is to us. Therefore, to grow in the stillness of the Lord's presence, it is essential to grow in the Word. As you grow in the Word, you will grow in the confidence of the great hymnist of old—the psalmist who found comfort in the presence of the Lord:

> *Where can I go from your Spirit? Where can I flee from your presence?*
> *If I go up to the heavens, you are there; if I make my bed in the depths, you are there.*
> *If I rise on the wings of the dawn, If I settle on the far side of the sea,*
> *even there your hand will guide me, your right hand will hold me fast.*
> *If I say, "Surely the darkness will hide me and the light become night around me,"*
> *even the darkness will not be dark to you; the night will shine like the day,*
> *for darkness is as light to you." (Psalm 139:7-12)*

DAY 26:

Our Journey

Monday, March 15, 2004

Dear Friends in Christ,

The sun is bursting in through the windows here at Theda Clark! For all my friends who feel they need to be somewhere warm this winter season, there is nothing like the bright sunrise on a crisp March morning! One week ago today, Kris began her intense rehab. What blessings the Lord has given us in one week. How many of us don't like to be weighed? We take that for granted. Last week, Kris could not stand on the scale and so had to be weighed on a lift. This week, she stood up from bed with no help, walked to the scale and stood on it. Last week, she could not sit by herself; today, she stands at the sink to bathe herself, brush her teeth, etc. Yesterday, she walked up four stairs. Side effects from medicines have cleared up. All this is due to one thing: the goodness of our God. Yesterday, a friend came to sit with Kris while I attended our Hmong worship service in Appleton. Twenty Hmong people were baptized. Twenty people received the gift of the Holy Spirit and all of God's blessings. It was at St. Paul's, which was my grandmother's church. I sat and remembered the many times as a young boy I stared up at the statue of Jesus with a little lamb on his shoulders. Nearly 40 years ago, when I sat with my grandmother, I had no idea where my life would take me. But, as I look back over 41 years, I have been that lamb on his shoulders—Kris has been that lamb, and so have all of us who trust in Christ as our Savior. Those baptisms remind us that our baptism was not a single event but it continues forward with lasting implications for our lives. We don't say, "I was baptized." We say: "I am baptized," as Paul says in Romans 6: "We were therefore buried with him through baptism into death in order that, just as Christ was raised from the dead through the glory of the Father, we too may live a new life." We have strength for the new week of rehab because we are baptized children of our Father.

God's blessings to you this day as we continue forward in our baptismal grace. Mark and Kris

DAY 26:

Your Journey

> "I know that my Redeemer lives, and that in the end he will
> stand upon the earth. And after my skin has been destroyed, yet
> in my flesh I will see God; I myself will see him with my own
> eyes—I, and not another. How my heart yearns within me!"
>
> JOB 19:25-27

How often we hear these verses! I use them at almost every funeral service because they offer great comfort and encouragement. But I don't think we often contemplate the context of Job's comments. Of course, we vaguely realize that they were spoken by Job somewhere in the midst of his great trials. He had lost his children, his possessions and his health. But look at the immediate context.

In verses 13-22, Job cries out in loneliness, observing that his family, close friends and acquaintances, and servants had all forsaken him. On top of that, his own physical suffering continued. Because of these things, he pleaded for pity from his friends. But most of his friends were not there, and the few who came to see him offered no comfort.

Listen to his words: "He has alienated my brothers from me; my acquaintances are completely estranged from me. My kinsmen have gone away; my friends have forgotten me. My guests and my maidservants count me a stranger; they look upon me as an alien. I summon my servant, but he does not answer, though I beg him with my own mouth. My breath is offensive to my wife; I am loathsome to my own brothers. Even the little boys scorn me; when I appear, they ridicule me. All my intimate friends detest me; those I love have turned against me. I am nothing but skin and bones; I have escaped with only the skin of my teeth. 'Have pity on me, my friends, have pity, for the hand of God has struck me. Why do you pursue me as God does? Will you never get enough of my flesh?'"

Have you ever had to say words of such deep despair? Job had sunk to a depth that can hardly be imagined by us. But out of this depth of "forsakenness" come to us some of the greatest words of hope and joy. No matter what loneliness, what separation, what "forsakenness" we face in life, the truth remains: our Redeemer lives. It is only when we deeply focus on the Lord's Passion that we remember that his Passion did not end at the cross or the tomb. His Passion became complete when he broke the bonds of the tomb and rose triumphant. The sweet songs of victory that we sing on Easter Sunday are not to be reserved for a Sunday or a season. Rather, they are the foundation of our lives and our source of hope and comfort. When we find our lives full of disappointment and loneliness, God calls us to lift up our eyes to the resurrection of our Lord and with great confidence say:

> *'Tis vain to trust in man; for Thou, Lord, only*
> *Art the Defense and Comfort of the lonely.*
> *With thee to lead, the battle shall be glorious*
> *And we victorious.*

> *(The Lutheran Hymnal 269)*

DAY 27:
Our Journey

Thursday, March 18, 2004

Dear Friends in Christ,

Rehab greetings from the 6th floor. Psalm 37:23 says: "If the Lord delights in a man's way, he makes his steps firm; though he stumble, he will not fall, for the Lord upholds him with his hand." Yesterday, Kris walked down the hall without the aid of the walker. Yes, it was true that the therapist was right behind her to steady her, but the fact is she did it. Yes, it is true that there were a few times that she stumbled. But the therapist's hand caught her. Really, it was the Lord through the therapist that caught her. As the passage says, sometimes we stumble in life, but we do not fall.

These past 36 days have merely been a stumble. But we have not fallen—fallen from grace that is—because the Lord's right hand has lifted us up. Why? Not because of us but because of the Lord's great mercy. In our nightly prayers, Kris and I always begin with our thanks to our Lord and our praise for his grace for the day. We also pray for you that His grace would be more and more evident every day to you.

My daughter went to Mel Gibson's movie *The Passion of Christ*, and before she went, I told her to remember that this happened to Jesus just for you. "Dad," she exclaimed afterwards, "I never knew they did all that beating." Yes, and he did it all for each one of us. Today, we head to the YMCA pool. We get to go swimming. For the first time in these 36 days, Kris will get to leave these walls. That in itself should be invigorating. Water therapy, here we come. Think of us at about 2:00 with a bunch of seniors doing water ballet! Meanwhile, we keep praying that Kris's muscles in her throat keep strengthening to pass her swallow test on Monday. It is amazing the things we have learned to pray for. Well, I wasn't going to write today but was lying in bed thinking of these things, and as I have said before, I write these things because they are therapeutic for me. I hope they are not too much of a nuisance for you. God's Blessings to you this day. Mark and Kris

DAY 27:

Our Journey

**"O LORD, do not forsake me; be not far from me, O my God.
Come quickly to help me, O Lord my Savior."**
PSALM 38:21

T hink of the times as a child when you knew that others had been invited to a party, and you were sitting home. You can probably still feel the loneliness— the rejection. As lonely as it can be not to be invited to a party, it is much worse to feel that God has left us.

It is easy to trust God and sing when the sun is shining, but what about during the testing time when the sun's light seems dimmed? I have seen people talk about their faith, but when the time of sorrow came upon them, they cried out in despair like those who have no hope. The psalmist above cried out to the Lord, too, but not in despair. He called out in great trust and confidence in the Lord. And what about Jesus? In spite of all his suffering, he never wavered in his trust. He still called God, "My God." He knew that God was still his—in the end, his father would be there for him. Job also said, "Though he slay me, I will trust in him."

Only a man of faith who understands the Lord's promises can claim those promises with confidence. Because our Lord was forsaken in our place, God has promised he will never forsake us. We can lay claim to those promises. Why? Because he is our LORD—the Savior God who has loved us so intensely. Jesus abhorred sin, he loathed sin, and his holy soul shrank from it. But on the cross, all our sins were laid upon Him. He willingly endured it. Why? Because he loved us.

Is there anyone who in the prime of life who would turn his back upon everything and die to save you? Jesus did. On Calvary, a man died, God died. He poured out a blood offering; he satisfied the law's demands. The moment we were brought into faith in Christ as our Savior, God said, "I see the blood; I don't see your sin. I will save you and keep you saved forever." This is what the Savior did for us. If he did—and since he did—can we not then also claim the promise of the Lord's presence in our lives? With the hymnist we also sing:

> *O God, forsake me not!*
> *Your gracious presence lend me;*
> *Lord, lead your helpless child;*
> *Your Holy Spirit send me*
> *That I my course may run.*
> *Oh, be my light, my lot,*
> *My staff, my rock, my shield—*
> *O God, forsake me not! (CW 424)*

DAY 28:

Our Journey

Saturday, March 20, 2004

Good Morning from Theda! God-willing this will be our last Saturday morning at Theda. We continue to look forward to a discharge sometime next week—possibly Wednesday. We know that we have to see the radiation doctor on Wednesday and begin planning for treatments. But, we have learned to take one day at a time. Our neurosurgeon came in yesterday and reported to us with great joy that the recent CAT scan showed almost no swelling in the brain. He is ready to discharge Kris from the hospital. The rehabilitation doctor is ready to discharge her. All that remains is our swallow test on Monday. Please pray with us that her throat muscles will strengthen and she will pass her test. However, we will deal with whatever the Lord gives us. Kris continues to do well, although the last two days they have really worked her. She needs a good weekend of rest and time with our daughters, who are coming today. Yesterday, I had a Mission Board meeting here at the hospital. I brought in Luigi's for the board as well as the staff. We also surprised Kris by bringing some pasta, and the speech therapist helped us puree it. We gathered around Kris's bed for our opening devotion and all sang together about the marvelous three-fold truth: Christ has died, Christ is risen, Christ will come again. We are reminded that the life, death, resurrection and his sure return have sustained us and give us the hope to fight each day's trials anew. Tomorrow is the Lord's Day. As you worship, praise God with us for these marvelous truths. Thanks for all your prayers, and I will report back Monday after her test.

God's Blessings
Mark and Kris

DAY 28:

Your Journey

"God sets the lonely in families."
PSALM 68:6

During my years of ministry, some of my best memories have come from ministering to aged Christians who find themselves separated from family and loved ones. These people just want to hear the Gospel and to be loved. They desire the joy of being in a family. So often, families forget those who are older. According to one social worker, more than half of the residents in a nursing home average only one phone call per month, and many go nearly a year without a visitor. A doctor once received a phone call from a young man who wanted to know how his mother was doing. "She died three years ago," the doctor had to inform the son. To aged Christians, when earthly families fail them, the Lord reminds them of the joy of the family of believers.

I remember one dear couple in Sturgeon Bay who had been married for more than 50 years. They remained best friends even when separated due to illness—he in a nursing home, she in a hospital, and no children left to console them. Yet, their faith remained unmovable because they were members of God's family and knew their Lord was with them. When I arrived in Tomahawk, there was a wonderful Christian lady who had been moved to Tomahawk, away from both her family and her hometown. It was as if she had been dumped there out of the way. But, the Lord set her into our family of believers, who loved her and shared Christ with her. At first, she talked about her loneliness for her home, her friends and her family. But the Lord replaced that loneliness with the joy of a new church family that loved her. I remember telling her that out of her loneliness, the Lord was able to provide an opportunity for many to show their faith.

Loneliness in others provides us the opportunity to step forward and provide a source of love, care and friendship. Sometimes we shrink back from such opportunities. We often bring our Sunday School children to visit nursing homes. I tell the children that they should not be afraid of the elderly. They may look different, not talk so well, but they have the same hopes and dreams—they just want to be loved. As we close this week of meditations on loneliness, let us remember that our Lord would have us see the loneliness others endure and step out of our lives to provide friendship and love. In love for those who are lonely, let us pray:

Holy Father, in Thy mercy Hear our anxious prayer;
Keep our loved ones who are absent
'Neath Thy Care

When in sorrow, When in loneliness
In Thy love look down and comfort
Their distress

May the joy of Thy salvation Be their strength and stay!
May they love and may they praise Thee
Day by Day

(The Lutheran Hymnal 643)

Week 5
Be Still in the Midst of Sickness

The devotions for "Your Journey" will lead us from Jesus' words from the cross, "I thirst" to encourage us to Be Still even in sickness.

DAY 29:

Our Journey

Monday, March 22, 2004

Dear Friends in Christ,

Good Morning from Theda Clark on Day 40. For Noah, it rained for 40 days and nights. Jesus spent 40 days in the wilderness. Kris has spent 40 days without eating "regular" food. Maybe today will be the end. Sometime today, she will have a swallow test. Please join us in praying that she will pass it. However, as Kris and I prayed last night, "Lord you know our wish, we would want to get beyond this and pass the test. But we will be content with whatever you will." In the whole scheme of things, this eating business is really minor, and we will take whatever comes today still rejoicing in God's goodness. I would like to share something very interesting. Our neurosurgeon came in on Saturday and gave Kris a gift-wrapped package. It was a beautiful picture of a man standing on a top of a very steep mountain peak overlooking the sunset. The title was the "the power of belief." It had a quote from Eleanor Roosevelt: "Believe in yourself. You gain strength, courage and confidence by every experience in which you stop to look fear in the face. You must do that which you think you cannot do." Our doctor has spoken to us about the importance of belief in a "higher power." But he need not share much because I have shared with him our faith in Jesus. He has walked in on us praying in the CCU waiting room. He has seen me in the chapel. While we thoroughly appreciate the devotion that this man has to his calling as a doctor and his attention and support of Kris and his thoughtfulness, we believe in more than ourselves. The power of our belief is in who we believe in: our Lord and Savior, Jesus. We have gained strength, courage and confidence from this experience because, as we have faced fear in the face, we fled to our Lord who has uplifted us by his mighty hand. We have done that which we cannot do because it is our Father in heaven who has worked in us his good pleasure and will. Our doctor is a great gift from God, but it is the Great Physician who has worked this miracle. At this point, we are on track to check out of our 6th floor rehab suite on Wednesday morning. We then have a lengthy consultation scheduled with the radiation oncologist on Wednesday. If Kris is not too tired, we will hit the road and head back home to paradise. Our hearts are getting excited, and we look forward to that day. This past weekend, I attended worship at the congregation where I grew up. The pastor was preaching a series on Job and was looking at Job 10. In the midst of his suffering, Job confesses that it is God who made him: "Your hands shaped me and made me.... Remember that you molded me like clay.... Did you not pour me out like milk and curdle me like cheese [this figurative language talking about development in the womb], clothe me with skin and flesh and knit me together with bones and sinews? You gave me life and showed me kindness, and in your providence watched over my spirit." Some may chose to believe that the marvelous human body just evolved over millions of years. With Job, Kris and I know that it is our God who made us in a unique way and gave us both body and soul. Through these last 40 days, our Lord has sustained both the body and soul of Kris. Throughout our lives, he has shown kindness extending way back to the day Jesus climbed the cross for our salvation and all those gifts became ours the day we were baptized. This has been a little wordy, but rejoice with us today that all of us are wondrously made and God's gift of salvation extends to us all. Believe in this, and you can look fear in the face and gain strength and courage. God's blessings to you this day. Oh—by the way, a number of people have wondered why I didn't report to you on our water ballet. It went beautifully. The "senior" ladies want to sign me up as long as I get a white swimming cap with a chin strap and goggles. It was good exercise for Kris, and we thought we should start a water ballet class in Tomahawk. Have a great day in the Lord and take time to stop and thank your Lord for his grace today. Mark and Kris

DAY 29:

Your Journey

"I thirst."
JOHN 19:28

Why did Jesus become human? Why did he take upon himself the form of man? Why didn't God send him full-grown into the world, and then let Him die for our sins? Why did he bring him through the womb of Mary and the stable of Bethlehem and the carpenter shop of Nazareth? Surely he came this way so that he might go through all the trials and difficulties of a human life, so that he could understand us and sympathize with us in all our trials and difficulties.

Who can help me most in my sorrow and sickness? Surely it is the one who has been through the same sorrow. Nothing will happen to us in the way of sorrow that did not happen to Jesus. He is the one we want when we need help and sympathy. The one who cried "I thirst" knows what suffering is, and he can help me when I suffer. Thank God, he knows all about us. He does care. He is touched with our grief. He knows when the sad heart aches till it nearly breaks. He knows when we have said goodbye to the dearest on earth. He knows, he cares, he sympathizes and he comforts.

Is your body racked with pain? So was His. Do you feel misunderstood? So was He. Have those who are nearest and dearest turned away from you? They did from him. Are you in the darkness? He was for three hours. He ran the gamut of all the suffering and the trials of all men, ending in his death on the cross and his awful cry of anguish, "I thirst."

When we suffer, we can go to him and pray, "Lord, you have suffered more than any man. I am suffering; I am going down into the sea of woe. Help me."

Never doubt that he will reach down from the cross, throw his arms around you and give you the peace that passes all understanding. Yes, the one who suffered most knows how to sympathize with us when we suffer. He knows what we face in life, and his cry expresses the deepest agony—one that we will never have to face. But while we do face our lesser sicknesses, our lesser agonies, we still have the confidence that we can turn to our Lord and Savior—our RISEN Lord and Savior—and know that he upholds us by his faithful promises and his mighty arm.

How firm a foundation, O saints of the Lord,
Is laid for your faith in his excellent Word!
What more can he say than to you he has said
Who unto the Savior for refuge have fled?

In ev'ry condition, in sickness, in health,
In poverty's vale, or abounding in wealth,
At home and abroad, on the land on the sea—
The Lord, the Almighty, your strength e'er shall be. (CW 416)

DAY 30:

Our Journey

Tuesday, March 23, 2004

Good Morning from Theda to all our dear friends in Christ,

Last week, I shared with you some thoughts from Matthew 5 during one of Kris's 3 a.m. snack times. Well, here I am again. Kris is snuggled nicely asleep, but my mind is just alive and thinking of all that has happened these 41 days. I was reminded of another note in my Bible on Matthew 5. This time, in this section on the salt and the light, Jesus says, "You are the salt of the earth.... You are the light of the world." I have penciled in this prayer, "Lord, keep me living while I am still alive." During these 41 days, I have seen people living even while dying, and I have seen people nearly dead though they were much alive. What I am saying is this: for us as Christians, Jesus doesn't say: You will become the salt and the light—rather, WE ARE. By virtue of faith in Jesus, we have been transformed. The guilt of sin and the sting of death have been taken away by our Lord. I have a standing joke with a dear friend about how we love guilt. But the glory of the Lutheran Christian faith really is and should always be that we are guilt-free. Once our dear Lord enters our hearts and makes us his own, we have his forgiveness, we have his love. Repentant—yes, we should be. But remember that repentance is part of our joyful living in Jesus. Living in forgiveness means we are the salt and the light. It means we "live for Jesus while still alive." I thank the Lord for these past 41 days. There have been some marvelous opportunities to witness— to be the salt and the light. As our time winds down here at Theda and these daily updates soon will end, I would like to just also thank my congregation in Tomahawk for being the salt and the light—for "living while still alive." For nearly 16 years, the Lord has privileged me by allowing me to serve as their shepherd. For many, I have been there with them through good and bad days. Now, they in love have been here for me. They have willingly allowed me to stay away from them these past 41 days to attend to Kris. They have done this in faith—they have reflected the love of the Lord in their lives—and they even have sent me a paycheck and more! I often joke with my fellow pastors when down in the valley that I am heading back to Paradise. It still isn't perfect, but my congregation and Tomahawk are our little bit of Paradise God has given to us on this earth. What a joy it will be for me this weekend to once again walk into the pulpit and share a special portion of God's Word with my family. My prayer is that all of you would have such a dear fellowship in your church family. Day 40 of our journey ended with Kris passing her swallow test. Her "fasting" is over and now to her is the sweet refreshment of a glass of water. Now to her is the ability to eat regular food. Does not the Lord continue to pour out his blessings? Yesterday, for Occupational Therapy, she did the wash. Today, she is going to make me lunch. Yes—I love these therapists for working on these domestic abilities! She is making sub sandwiches and a fruit dish. I told her I expect this to be by candlelight with a little wine. We also plan on walking down to the CCU unit. I remember the nurses saying that they rarely see the healthy ones. So, we are going to have Kris walk in and give them our thanks. Well, I have probably spoken too much already. I'm still not sure I can sleep yet because my mind is just full of all the good things the Lord has placed before us. I have learned and relearned many lessons these past 41 days. But what we can all take away from this experience is that no matter what our situation in life, let's keep living while still alive.

God's Blessings to you this day.

Mark and Kris

DAY 30:

Your Journey

**Later, knowing that all was now completed, and
so that the Scripture would be fulfilled,
Jesus said, "I am thirsty."**
JOHN 19:28

Which words of Jesus from the cross provide you the most comfort? When you see him asking for forgiveness for those who are persecuting him, it reminds you that the Lord intercedes for our forgiveness. When you see him opening the doorway of heaven to the thief on the cross, you are reminded that heaven is open for you, too. As he provides for his mother, so he provides for you. Hearing his cry of intense separation makes you realize that you will never be separated from God. His cry announcing that his work is done gives us the sure hope that our salvation is done. His final cry from the cross, "Father, into your hands I commend my spirit" has become the parting words for many Christians. Which of these provides the greatest comfort? But wait— there is one more—one that is often overlooked. "I thirst" was Jesus' only cry concerning physical pain. Let us look more closely at this often-overlooked word from the cross.

Jesus' fifth statement from the cross is also the shortest. In the original Greek language, it is only one word of four letters. Yet, when we study this word of Christ in its setting, when we remember who Jesus is and why he said, "I thirst," then this short gasp becomes a mighty big and comforting word.

Christ uttered these words at the end of his crucifixion. According to experts, death by crucifixion was the most painful mode of torture ever conceived by man. With the loss of blood and the amount of sweating, Jesus also experienced dehydration along with the other pains of the crucifixion. Hunger is painful, but it is nothing compared to the pangs of thirst. Psalm 22 describes the intense thirst Jesus experienced on the cross: "My strength is dried up like a potsherd [piece of broken pottery], and my tongue sticks to the roof of my mouth." Look at what Jesus has been through, and there is no wonder that our Lord cried out. Eighteen to twenty hours before this moment, our Lord was in the Garden praying so intensely that his sweat was like great drops of blood. He was taken captive. All night long, he alternated between being on trial and being used as a punching bag by the soldiers. Beaten and bruised, he was hauled before Pilate. He was sentenced, ridiculed, scourged, crowned with thorns and forced to carry his cross. He was hung from long, rough spikes piercing through his hands and feet. The wood of the cross ground into his back. No wonder he finally cried out, "I thirst."

Try going several hours without drinking anything. Feel how your tongue sticks to the roof of your mouth, how your strength is dried up. For hours upon hours, our Lord faced Satan without the smallest droplet of water. But why? He did this for you and for me. As we contemplate Jesus' painful thirst, we look at the words of the old hymn and pray:

Jesus, in thy thirst and pain, While thy wounds thy life-blood drain,
Thirsting more our love to gain: Hear us Holy Jesus.

Thirst for us in mercy still, All thy holy work fulfill,
Satisfy thy loving will: Hear us Holy Jesus.

May we thirst thy love to know; Lead us in our sin and woe
Where the healing waters flow: Hear us Holy Jesus (The Lutheran Hymnal 184)

DAY 31:

Our Journey

Wednesday, March 24, 2004

Dear Friends in Christ,

Today is day 42. This is the day the Lord has made, let us rejoice and be glad in it! We have waited patiently for the Lord to say, "This is the day." And today it is—WE ARE OUT OF HERE! We are hitting the road; we are busting out and heading home! So ends this part of our journey. With the psalmists, we have cried unto the Lord, and he has heard our prayer. Before we go, I must thank all of you for permitting me to share our journey with you, and I praise God that so many of you have walked with us to the throne of our gracious God and carried our burdens and our joys to our heavenly Father. So many of you expressed it, but one of my friends from way out West spoke of how he had never been to Neenah, never seen Theda Clark, but was hanging around the edges in prayer. Do you remember the dream I shared with you way back early in our journey? I was sitting on the couch in the CCU waiting room and behind me was this large gathering of people, some I knew and some I didn't. That was you, and what a joy to our hearts to know that you have been with us. Following the example of Paul, I don't just simply thank you, but more—I thank God for you! God has blessed us through your many words of encouragements. I would especially like to thank so many of my brother pastors who came to share God's Word with me. Some of them came often and were great sources of strength. It is amazing that in all the devotions that were shared with Kris and me, not one pastor ever repeated the same portion of God's Word. That shows us the depths of God's counsel and comfort from his Word. Brothers in the ministry—I have been blessed by your ministering to us! A word concerning these e-mails: when I began these, I had no idea that the Lord would take these reports to you in the direction He took them. If in some small way the Lord has used them to strengthen you, praise him and give glory to his name, and I thank him that he has used me as his instrument. These were borne out of the crucible of suffering and are not easily repeated. Therefore, they will come to an end, but God's Word does not. However, from time to time, I will share with you Kris's progress and our future treatments. One small account before I end: There was a lady who was brought into CCU shortly before Kris was moved upstairs. I think I talked to you about the hopelessness I saw in the eyes of her loved ones. I spoke to them several times and prayed with them. They had no church—no foundation to grasp. Sometime later when I visited them, I walked in as they were reading one of the Psalms I had recommended. Someday, if I see them in heaven, this will have all been worth it. Today we leave. We first of all stop for an appointment with the radiation doctor. Although this segment of our journey is over, we still must press forward through other trials. At this point, we anticipate radiation to begin right after Easter, unless the radiation doctor sees the need to begin sooner. But we look at today and let the Lord worry about tomorrow. Today we will leave these walls behind. Today we will go home to our daughters and to our church family. Today, if our strength holds out, we will walk into our Lenten Meditation and join our family in praising the Lord for his goodness. Wherever you may be worshipping this evening, join us in praising him. The last song we sang in Tomahawk before we left was "On Eagles' Wings." He has lifted us up on the healing wings of our great Savior whose passion we celebrate this Lenten season. He lifts you up as well through faith in Jesus. Hallelujah, Praise the Lord—we are out of here! God's Blessings, Mark and Kris

DAY 31:

Your Journey

"As the deer pants for streams of water, so
my soul pants for you, O God.
My soul thirsts for God, for the living God.
Where can I go and meet with God?"
PSALM 42:1-2

We have been focusing on the "Stillness of the Lord," as I call it. That stillness stems from those great words in Psalm 46, "Be still, and know that I am God." Just stop, be silent, be still—and see the Lord filling your life with living water. We spend so much time wondering why some sickness, sorrow or crisis has entered our lives. We spend so much effort on trying to find the cause of our troubles or the person who's to blame. Politicians and news reporters want to point the finger. Quarrels between couples sap energy as each tries to blame the others. Such negative energy is destructive—especially when that negative energy leads to blaming God.

Instead, let us focus our energy on the results. In all problems of life, our Lord would lead us to "pant after him." The psalmist points out how the deer pants for water. Even more so, when sorrows or conflicts overtake our lives, let us thirst for that which can truly quench our thirst. Let us be still before the Lord and know that he will fill our mouths, our lives, our souls with that living water that is always fresh.

There have been any number of times that I have stopped by a member's house and they have said, "Pastor, I am so glad you stopped, I have been waiting for you to share a little word with me. I need some comfort from God's Word." Often, I visit someone the night before their surgery and give them the Lord's Supper. They not only need it—they *want* that spiritual food. They are "panting" after the Lord.

Our problem is that we "pant" for many other things of life that do not fill us up. I love a good salad. But an hour later, I am hungry again. Earthly treasures are like salads. They do not fill us up. Living in the stillness of the Lord is to remove the frantic searching for the things of the world and take time to listen to our Savior. Oftentimes, it takes some kind of sickness or trial in life to slow us down and let us be still and be filled with the living water of his love and forgiveness and his care and concern.

As pants the heart for cooling streams When heated in the chase,
So longs my soul, O God, for Thee And thy refreshing grace.

For Thee, my God, the living God, My thirsty soul doth pine;
Oh, when shall I behold thy face, Thou Majesty Divine?

(The Lutheran Hymnal 525)

DAY 32:

Our Journey

Friday, March 26, 2004

Dear Friends in Christ,

Hello from Tomahawk! Two nights in our own bed! How wonderful to be back here in our home. We arrived home at about 3 p.m. on Wednesday to signs and balloons. We walked into church on Wednesday evening greeted by so many family members. It was wonderful to see so many in worship. Kris and I greeted people afterwards, and I think Kris stood for over 1/2 hour. We started PT and OT in Tomahawk yesterday and will continue up until Easter. Following Easter, Kris will have a three- to four-day stay in the hospital for a special kind of radiation treatment, during which she will have to stay in a special room with very limited visitors. On April 19, she will begin 14 outpatient radiation treatments, ending on May 6. We will then determine if further treatment is needed. I just wanted to send this little note to you to let you know what is happening and how much we appreciate all the expressions of love and support. This weekend, I will be having a special worship service in Tomahawk (naturally all of you are invited), and I will focus on a phrase that came about during our stay. We received several cards with generous gifts of money inside, and they were signed: "Just in Time." My sermon this weekend will be "Just in Time," focusing on various passages from Galatians 4 and 6. I may send the sermon to you once I have preached it. There were so many things that happened "Just in Time" during our stay, but the most important thing that happened is that our Lord Jesus appeared "just in time" some 2,000 years ago to be our Savior. Wherever you worship this weekend, may you praise your Lord and our Lord for all of his goodness "just in time." God's Blessings this weekend. Mark and Kris

DAY 32:

Your Journey

**"The Lord is my Shepherd.... He leads me beside
quiet waters, he restores my soul."**
PSALM 23:1-3

A young man once stopped me after a church service and asked, "Pastor, how did you do it? How did you get through all your challenges?" My answer: "The Lord did—the Lord did it here!" I was referring to God's House. Every Sunday, when I gathered for worship, the Lord was leading me beside quiet waters. Every time I ran to his Word for comfort and counsel, he was restoring my soul. Every time around Word and Sacrament is a meal from our Savior that nourishes, strengthens and fortifies our souls.

The Lord often draws us back to his Word during times of sickness. We may view times of sickness as bad times. Rather, let us remember that through those times our Lord may be accomplishing some wondrous and gracious things for us or for others.

I am reminded of my good friend, Dick. Dick has had five back operations. Most people would look at that as a bad thing. However, Dick said to me, "The Lord had to throw me on my back to make me look up to him—and it has taken five times." Dick is a wonderful Christian and a great man of the Word. While his body continues to suffer the effects of his injuries, God often leads him to quiet waters and restores his soul with the promises of Jesus.

Peter reminds us of this in his epistle: "Praise be to the God and Father of our Lord Jesus Christ! In his great mercy he has given us new birth into a living hope through the resurrection of Jesus Christ from the dead, and into an inheritance that can never perish, spoil or fade—kept in heaven for you, who through faith are shielded by God's power until the coming of salvation that is ready to be revealed in the last time. In this you greatly rejoice, though now for a little while you may have had to suffer grief in all kinds of trials. These have come so that your faith—of greater worth than gold, which perishes even though refined by fire—may be proved genuine and may result in praise, glory and honor when Jesus Christ is revealed." (1 Peter 1:3-7)

Yes, we do face all kinds of trials, including sicknesses, but through it all, our Lord leads us to quiet waters and restores our souls.

Once again, we are reminded of this through the great hymn:

Savior, I follow on, Guided by thee, Seeing not yet the hand That leadeth me.
Hushed be my heart and still; Fear I no further ill. Only to meet thy will My will shall be.

Riven the rock for me, Thirst to relieve, Manna from heaven falls Fresh every eve.
Never a want severe Causeth my eye a tear, But thou dost whisper near, "Only believe."(CW 473)

DAY 33:

Our Journey

Thursday, April 8, 2004

Dear Friends in Christ,

Hello from warm Tomahawk! We are in the midst of Holy Week, and most of our thoughts are on the love of Jesus in his suffering and death for us. However, we have often thought of all of you who have supported and prayed for us. For many days we were connected via cyberspace. I thought that some of you might be interested in how we are doing. Last Thursday, Kris's MRI and CAT scan showed no sign of returning tumor or other cancer. Now we are back in Tomahawk. Thursday, Friday and Saturday are big days for us, not just because I am a pastor, but because they mean so much to us and to our faith. Many have asked us how we endured 42 days in the hospital. The answer lies not within us or any person. It is found in the power of the cross of our Savior and in the joy of the empty tomb. This Easter, when we sing, "I know that my Redeemer lives," these will not be just empty words. Those words remind us that our Savior is powerful enough to break the bonds of death and to accomplish our salvation. This same Savior promises to walk with us during each and every trial. He has walked with us and sustained us. He offers the same for you. My dear friends, I have wanted to take some time to personally write so many of you, but time is just slipping away. But this is my prayer for you: that you would be in worship in God's House this Thursday, Friday and Sunday. When you are in worship, along with a prayer for us, pray with us for you that God would strengthen even more our love of our Savior. Mel Gibson may give us a visual image of our suffering Savior. But it is the precious Word of our God that will be the foundation for our journey through this life. This past Sunday, we had a funeral for a lady from my congregation. I encouraged the family that Harriett will be spending Easter with Jesus. But our joy is that we can spend Easter with Jesus here as we worship in His House. This is our prayer for you. After spending an Easter meal with our children, we will head to the Appleton area. On Monday, Kris will begin her first radiation treatment. This is a special radiation inserted right into a capsule in her head. Although she should not suffer any effects, due to the radioactive nature of this medicine, she will be hospitalized at Appleton Medical Center until Friday morning with limited visitors. I can only see her an hour a day. But our Lord will spend 24/7/365 with her, and he is the Great Physician. The following Monday, we then begin 14 whole-brain radiation treatments. God-willing, May 6 will be the last of her treatments. Dear friends, the night is getting late, and I think I now have most items set for my worship services. What remains are some small items to do. What really remains is to simply enjoy the riches of God's grace these next several days. May you also truly enjoy these days! God's Blessings, Mark and Kris

DAY 33:

Your Journey

**"Come to me, all you who are weary and
burdened, and I will give you rest."**
MATTHEW 11:28

In most cases, worrying about something does more damage to the worrier than the actual thing itself does. In fact, modern medical research has proven that worry breaks down resistance to disease. More than that, it actually diseases the nervous system—particularly that of the digestive organs and the heart. Surely, Jesus knew this when he encouraged in his Sermon on the Mount: "Do not worry.... Who of you by worrying can add a single hour to his life?"

In 1929, retail giant J. C. Penney was almost crippled by worry. With business highly unstable, he spent his nights awake, worrying, and soon contracted shingles. In the hospital, Penney was treated with tranquilizing medicine, but it was no help. He still worried. One night, fearing that he would die before morning, he began writing farewell letters to his wife, son and friends. But the next morning, as he was lying in bed, he heard singing from the hospital chapel next door: "No matter what may be the test, God will take care of you...." Suddenly, he leaped up, thinking: "It is real! God loves and cares for me." In no time, he had jumped out of his bed and entered the chapel. He stated that it was if he were a little bird suddenly freed to fly out of the dungeon into the sunlight, from hell to paradise.

There was once a little girl who was taken to the doctor for a minor but painful operation. When all was ready, the kindly doctor said, "This will hurt, but you may cry or scream as much as you please." The little girl looked up at him, smiling, and said, "I would rather sing," which she did with her sweet, childish voice, passing through her brief ordeal without a sigh, groan or tear.

The passage from Matthew above is a special verse of mine. I often share it with people in the hospital or in the midst of crisis. Living in the stillness of the Lord means that we also see Jesus in this special light. Picture Jesus, as I do, standing there with his arms outstretched. Those eyes—those eyes that emanate love more than any eyes ever created—beam on us with compassion. Those hands are soft and smooth, while his arms are strong to carry. "Come to me," Jesus beckons. "Come with all your sins, all your temptations, all your hardships, your sicknesses and diseases, your sorrows and your cares; drop them at my feet and let me take care of it."

I heard the voice of Jesus say, "Come unto me and rest; Lay down, O weary one, lay down Your head upon my breast."
I came to Jesus as I was, Weary and worn and sad; I found in him a resting place, And he has made me glad.

I heard the voice of Jesus say, "Behold, I freely give The living water, thirsty one; Stoop down and drink and live."
I came to Jesus, and I drank Of that life-giving stream; My thirst was quenched, my soul revived,
And now I live in him. (CW 338)

DAY 34:

Our Journey

Saturday, April 17, 2004

Dear Friends in Christ,

Good Saturday morning. I just came in from a beautiful morning run. I ran along the river and just marveled at the Lord's goodness. How was your Easter? Even though Holy Week was very hectic with more last-minute prep than usual, it was just good to be home. But what was better is that we once again were able to sing, "He is risen" on Easter morning. In a card that I gave Kris on Easter morning, I wrote, "This Easter is special more importantly because we are worshipping the risen Savior, but on top of that he woke you up." Tomorrow is another celebration of Easter—in fact, every Sunday is. This past week, Kris had her first round of treatments with the "isotope injection." She had to be secluded in a room from Monday to Thursday. I brought to her the two grocery bags full of cards that we had received. One bag she had not been able to see since they came while she was sleeping. She was able to read them all during her four days. She was astonished by all these expressions of love. When you all sent those cards while she was sleeping, did you think that the Lord would use them for reading material while she was undergoing this procedure? He works everything out in His plan. When they finished the procedure on Thursday, the nurse remarked that she has never had someone do so well as Kris on this treatment. Does that surprise us? God has been so good and gracious that once again he watched over her. On Easter Sunday, one of our common refrains during worship was "This is the day the Lord has made, let us rejoice and be glad in it." Whether your day is filled with sadness or with happiness, tears or laughter, rejoice and be glad that you have a Savior that walks with you as he walks with us. We rest confidently in Him as we begin the second round of treatments on Monday. During the week, Kris will stay with her mother in New London, and she will have radiation treatment every day at 10 a.m. for 14 days. She will come home on the weekends. God willing, on May 6, I will pick her up at 10:30 a.m., and we will head home with treatments concluded. Well, just wanted to update you and thank you all again for your prayers. God's Blessings on your worship tomorrow. Mark and Kris

DAY 34:

Your Journey

**"If the Lord delights in a man's way, he makes
his steps firm; though he stumble,
he will not fall, for the Lord upholds him with his hand."**
PSALM 37:23

W hile Kris was learning to walk all over again, there were times of stumbling. But our Lord held her up. We did not fall from grace. God upheld us by his powerful hand. Have you stumbled? What is it that is causing you to trip on your journey of life? We all do, but we do not fall from grace. Why?

Jesus stumbled under the cross, but he did not fall from his task of accomplishing our salvation. Though weakened and bruised, he did not give up but was upheld by the power of God. It was his extreme love for us that motivated him to endure to the end. This grace is what holds us up, as the hymnist declares:

It was grace in Christ that called me, Taught my darkened heart and mind, Else the world had yet enthralled me, To your heavenly glories blind. Now I worship none above you; For your grace alone I thirst, Knowing well that, if I love you, You, O Father, loved me first.
(The Lutheran Hymnal 37)

In the Psalms, God's Old Testament people are constantly told to remember—remember how God brought them up out of Egypt. Remember how God brought them up from bondage and gave them their own country, where they could live in freedom before the Lord.

Our Egypt—our bondage—is slavery to sin, death and the devil. Yet the Lord rescued us and brought us into his kingdom—his family of believers. Being part of

144

the family of believers—the invisible church—implies special blessings. It is a glorious thing to be a part of the church—the body of Christ—His family. In this family, we have received God's grace. A long-forgotten hymn speaks to us today about the glorious blessings of being in Christ's family:

Glorious things of Thee are spoken, Zion, city of our God; He whose word cannot be broken Formed thee for his own abode. On the Rock of Ages founded, What can shake thy sure repose? With salvation's walls surrounded, Thou may'st smile at all thy foes.

See, the streams of living water Springing from eternal love Well supply thy sons and daughters and all fear of want remove. Who can faint while such a river Ever flows their thirst to assuage—Grace, while like the Lord, the Giver, Never fails from age to age?

(The Lutheran Hymnal 369)

DAY 35:

Our Journey

Monday, April 18, 2004

Five down—nine to go. That is the status of our radiation treatments. Sunday's message in worship was based on the vision of John in Revelation as he was permitted to look into the throne room of heaven and see the Lamb of God—our Savior—sitting there worthy of all praise and honor because he was slain for our freedom. Even in the midst of our trials, we can sing our songs of hope—a sure and living hope that He will not let us down. As God always does—whether a sunny day or rainy day—he smiles upon us with his love and mercy. He continues to do that during these treatments. With two weeks behind us, we have nine more days. We thank you for your continued prayers. Also, here is Kris to share some thoughts with you:

Hi everyone. I am so blessed to have so many good friends, and I thank you for everything. Having had cancer four times in the last four years, I am so thankful for all who have supported me. This year, by God's grace, I will be walking in the Tomahawk Relay for Life. It wasn't so long ago that I was wondering if I would walk without aid. But God has brought me so far. The Relay for Life helps in the fight against cancer by funding research. I really hesitate to ask, but several of you have already volunteered, and Mark said that I should. So, I thought I would just let you know, and if you want to support me in the Relay for Life, here is what happens. In case you don't know, participants in the relay are divided up into teams. I am on Team Favor's Birthday. For several months before the relay, teams do different things to raise funds. Then, on the night of the relay, there is a big area that we walk around, and there are bags with names on them in memory of individuals and speakers and singers, etc. Many teams camp out overnight. If you would like to support me in my walking for cancer research, you can send any amount to my address by May 25. I won't feel bad if you don't or if you are helping others, so it is totally up to you. Tomorrow I head to Appleton for my second week of radiation. So far all seems OK. They say that this week I may start feeling fatigued. I am staying with my mom during the week and come home on the weekends. Thanks to all. Kris and Mark

DAY 35:

Your Journey

**"Come, you who are blessed by my Father; take your inheritance....
I was thirsty and you gave me something to drink....
Whatever you did for one of the least of these
brothers of mine, you did for me."**
MATTHEW 25:34–35, 40

O
ur Lord died in physical thirst. But we are spiritually alive, never again to face eternal thirst. Our souls are refreshed and replenished. Our Lord has done this. Now, our Lord asks us to look beyond ourselves.

To live in the stillness of the Lord helps us to look beyond ourselves because we are looking up to our Savior. We see our Savior's love not just for us, but for the world. The water of salvation that has filled our souls abounds for us to share. Is there someone today in your life that needs a glass of water? Do they need physical help? Then reach out your hand. More importantly, are they spiritually thirsty? Then reach out your love and fill them with the same good news of our Savior that now fills your soul.

At Christmas time, I often wonder how the people of Bethlehem reacted to the proclamation of the shepherds. The Bible tells us that the shepherds "returned, glorifying and praising God for all the things they had heard and seen." They could not keep quiet because their hearts had been filled. They had gone to see the Savior, and now they beheld their salvation.

Every time we gather for worship, the Lord is pouring out into our hearts and souls his living water of forgiveness and salvation. The more we take, the more we are refreshed. As the hymn below states, these words are: "bread life-giving," "light" and "sword prevailing." They bring us the greatest joy.

Let our prayer be that as the Word of God nourishes our souls, we, in joy, also return, glorifying and praising God for all that we have seen.

Lord, your words are water living Where I quench my thirsty needs.
Lord, your words are bread life-giving, On your words my spirit feeds.
Lord, your words will be my light Through death's cold and dreary night,
Yes they are my sword prevailing And my cup of joy unfailing.

As I pray, dear Jesus, hear me; Let your words in me take root.
May your Spirit e'er be near me That I bear abundant fruit.
May I daily sing your praise, From my heart glad anthems raise,
Till my highest praise is given In the endless joy of heaven.

(CW 283)

Week 6

Be Still in the Midst of Uncertainty

The devotions for "Your Journey" will lead us from Jesus' words from the cross, "It is finished" to encourage us to Be Still even during life's uncertainties.

DAY 36:

Our Journey

Saturday, May 8, 2004

Dear Friends in Christ,

As we approach Mother's Day, I thought it would be good to update you on Kris's progress. Sitting on my desk—no not Kris—but sitting on my desk is a little rose that we are handing out this weekend in worship. Our worship this weekend will focus on mothers and the gift of life. "Cherish the Roses of Life—a Daughter, a Mother, a Wife. Their smile, their strength and their love like blessings sent down from above." Living in a world that seems to value life less and less, faced with terrorists who care not who is killed and with many individuals who would rather hurt you than help you, the precious gift of life stands out all the more. Our message this weekend is a continuation of a series of messages during this Easter season from the book of Revelation. Before us is the vision of heaven in Rev. 21. In my stack of Mother's Day items is one article entitled "Christian because of a Mother." How true that is, that God has used countless mothers to pass on the faith to their children. This weekend, we are grateful for all those Christian mothers, and our home is grateful for our Christian mother whom God woke up so she can still be there for her children. Yesterday, I brought Kris home from New London after completing her 14th and last radiation treatment. Her mother has been a wonderful source of help and blessing while Kris stayed with her during these last 2 1/2 weeks. At the present, her head is really sore, and you can see that it is red from the treatments. But she is finished, and all seems to be well. She has a period of rest now until the end of the month when we have testing and doctor's appointments. We pray that all will be well and no further treatments will be necessary. How often Kris and I have been thankful for all of you who have stood beside us in our hour of trial in prayer. God's blessings to you this weekend. Mark and Kris

DAY 36:

Your Journey

"When he had received the drink, Jesus said, 'It is finished.'"
JOHN 19:30

On Wednesday, March 24, 2004, I wrote my last e-mail from Theda Clark. "Dear Friends in Christ, Today is day 42. This is the day the Lord has made, let us rejoice and be glad in it! We have waited patiently for the Lord to say, 'This is the day.' And today it is—WE ARE OUT OF HERE!" We were finished with our stay in the hospital—but we were not really finished with our fight against cancer. The fight went on. Was Jesus' cry from the cross, "It is finished," filled with the same meaning? Was he saying, "I'm out of here"? No—his use of the word was different, and thanks be to God that it was.

Jesus' final statement—one word in Greek—was one of triumph. He had won. He had done it. His word shouted out to the world that He had reached the fulfillment. Here is the climax of the greatest story ever written, the central point of a story written by God, the deciding point of a true story around which centers the welfare of the entire human race.

The very moment that God confronted Adam and Eve in their sin, he set into motion his plan of salvation. He announced that a seed of the woman—one of her descendants—would come and crush Satan. Throughout the Old Testament, our gracious God continued to offer his promise of the coming Savior. Day after day, the Jews sacrificed animal after animal on the altar of God. Each repeated sacrifice was a visual reminder that one day there would be ONE sacrifice that would really count— it would really pay for all sins and it would not need to be repeated. The prophets held before God's people visions of this sacrifice—it would be God's Son. He would be born of a virgin. He would be born in Bethlehem. He would be rejected by his own people. He would be a suffering servant. People would turn away from him. One of his own disciples would betray him. His other disciples would desert him. Even God the Father would forsake him. Yet, he would still be victorious. He would win.

Now here it was. On the cross, the struggle between Christ and his archenemy, the devil, reached its height. One or the other had to go down in defeat. If Jesus had failed at this crucial moment, his story—and ours—would be a tragedy, and the Bible would be the saddest book ever written. But Jesus' final word is not a word of failure. Christ cries out in triumph. He won the victory—and, with him, we, too, have won the victory.

Jesus, all our ransom paid, All your Father's will obeyed,
By your sufferings perfect made: Hear us, holy Jesus!

Save us in our soul's distress, Be our Help to cheer and bless
While we grow in holiness: Hear us, holy Jesus.

Brighten all our heavenward way With an ever holier ray
Till we pass to perfect day: Hear us, holy Jesus
(The Lutheran Hymnal 185)

DAY 37:

Our Journey

One Year Later

To Kris's Mom and Sisters and Family,

I'm not sure this is the best way to update you, but right now, it is the most expedient way. As we leave today for vacation, Kris is considerably weaker than two weeks ago. Over the past two weeks, I have seen an unfortunate decline in Kris's energy level. I have been wanting to share some information with you for some time. At the recent doctor's appointment, it became apparent that the cancer is growing. Kris and I have not necessarily shared just exactly where the cancer is because we didn't want to cause panic when we still had many options available. Now we are down to one form of chemo that the doctor will use when we get back. To be honest, the doctor does not hold out much hope for this chemo either. All that the chemo has done is slow the rate of growth of the cancer. It has not stopped it. It continues to grow, and her cells are becoming resistant to chemo. I don't wish to depress you right now, but I think I should share with you honestly where the cancer is. The cancer has gone into her liver. There are several spots that continue to grow. There is also some cancer between her liver and stomach. Now, her recent episode shows more down near her bladder. Unfortunately, it is only a matter of time before the cancer begins to affect the function of the liver. Once that happens, it is only in the Lord's hands as far as what will progress. The radiation doctor said that when liver functions become affected, it could take as little as two weeks for that to cause the end of life. At any rate, I think we should be prepared for realizing that we could be in the last year of Kris's life. I write this with great sorrow because I know how it affects me and my daughters and I know the sorrow that will fill your heart as you read this. But, you are such an important part of Kris's life that I think you might want to know this. Understand that I am not giving up, but hard facts are staring me in the face. Kris has been talking more and more that she feels this is different than before, and she is beginning to talk more and more about the end of life. I am not sure if she always understands everything the doctor says, and up until now I have always talked with her about improving. After vacation, I think we will have some more focused discussions. We are waiting for a call from the doctor this morning because we may even have to stop and visit him on the way to Milwaukee. Kris just isn't rebounding like she has in the past. Deb—if you think it best, you can also share this with your mom. I've been wanting to talk to her but I just haven't been able to find the time or the words. Kris worries so much about her, and she often is filled with guilt to cause people pain, which of course I remind her that it is not her fault or anyone's. Once again, I want to let you know that our home is always open to you to visit. I'm not sure what this chemo will do to her, but as much as possible, I will want you to be able to visit with Kris. We plan on stopping in at Waupaca on the 17th for Pat's birthday. We get off the plane at 1:30 and so I would think we could be in Waupaca around 4:00. Well, I am sure I could say more, but I think you have the picture. My eyes are filled with tears right now just thinking of you receiving this, and I am sorry if this is not the right way to share this with you, but you are all way too important to not share this with you. Yesterday, in our psalm reading we read from Psalm 119, which says: "It was good for me to be afflicted so that I may learn your decrees." As Christians, we view suffering not as bad, but we know that our Lord can bring good out of all things. The key is that we turn to him during this time and find counsel and comfort in His word. Let us not become bitter because that would be falling into Satan's temptation. But let us even more cling to the promises and mercy of our gracious Savior. God-willing, we will see you all on the 17th. Mark

DAY 37:

Your Journey

"When he had received the drink, Jesus said, 'It is finished.'"
JOHN 19:30

W e are now in the last week of our journey in the stillness of the Lord. From Psalm 46:10 ("Be still, and know that I am God") through the various promises of the Old Testament to the words of our dying Savior from the cross, we have seen how we can be still in the midst of our trials and troubles. But, we are also reminded that no problem or challenge, no strife or stress, no trial or trouble, no illness or disease could ever be greater than what our Lord endured on the cross. Through it all, our Lord was still in the confidence that he was in the hands of his heavenly Father. Toward the end of his suffering, Jesus asked for a drink. That little drink could not have completely quenched his thirst, but it did water his mouth enough to enable him to utter another word. And it was literally *a* word: *tetelestai*, Greek for "It is finished."

What does this mean? What is finished? Is his life finished? Is the crucifixion finished? Is our Lord finished? He most certainly is not!

Just the opposite! *Tetelestai* shouts Jesus' victory. It means, "It is finished, it stands finished and it always will be finished!" While it is true that our Lord's sufferings were now finished, there is much more included in this dramatic word. Many of the Old Testament types and prophecies were now fulfilled, and the once-for-all sacrifice for sin had now been completed.

One of my favorite hymns is "He's Risen, He's Risen." In verse two, we sing: "The foe was triumphant when on Calvary The Lord of creation was nailed to the tree. In Satan's domain did the hosts shout and jeer, For Jesus was slain, whom the evil ones fear." This is true, but then listen to verse three: "But short was their triumph; the Savior arose, And death, hell and Satan, he vanquished, his foes." While it is most certainly true that the resurrection proved to us that our Savior won, yet it was on the cross that our Lord fought the battle, and it was on the cross that he won. This word from the cross was the shout of victory from the battlefield: "I have defeated Satan, I have defeated sin, I have paid for hell, I have purchased heaven." Our Lord shouted out to all with this word. It is this word that provides us the greatest stillness in all uncertainty of life. It is this word that encourages our faith. It is this word that inspired the hymn writer:

The Sixth, when victory was won,
"Tis finished!" for thy work was done.
Grant, Lord, that, onward pressing
We may the work Thou dost impose
Fulfill with Thine own blessing.

(The Lutheran Hymnal 177)

DAY 38:

Our Journey

June 17, 2005

Dear Friends in Christ,

Over a year ago, you joined us on an incredible journey—a journey of faith and confidence in the Lord's enduring promises. That journey was and is based upon Psalm 46. Before I share the latest on Kris, let us just be reminded of that great Psalm: "God is our refuge and strength, an ever-present help in trouble. Therefore we will not fear, though the earth give way and the mountains fall into the heart of the sea, though its waters roar and foam and the mountains quake with their surging. There is a river whose streams make glad the city of God, the holy place where the Most High dwells. God is within her, she will not fall…. Be still, and know that I am God…. The Lord Almighty is with us; the God of Jacob is our fortress." The reason I share that Psalm is because I saw that confidence in Kris yesterday morning while hospitalized here at Appleton Medical Center. Three weeks ago, Kris developed some complications. On the 9th, we were scheduled to leave for a family vacation, which we did. But, Kris continued to grow weaker, and we came back home early this past Tuesday. Further testing has shown that the cancer is aggressively increasing. We knew this day was going to come, and now it has. Today, we will be leaving AMC and driving home to Tomahawk and will enter into the hospice program. No more chemo, but what is left is comfort care for Kris. Our girls are coming back from the rest of vacation today and joining us in New London for Kris's mother's birthday and then on home to Tomahawk. What quiet confidence the Lord has placed into Kris. With calmness and a living hope in her Savior, she talks openly about the ending of life and her new life in heaven. With the attitude that she lies in the hands of her Savior, she wants to "set her house in order." I know not every day will be calm, and we all have our moments. But at times like this, we can stand back and be inspired by the Lord's guiding faith in the heart of one of his children. God is her refuge. Does she fear—do we all? We have those anxious moments but fear—true fear—has been driven away because our Lord has assured us that there remains a more glorious home for us. We cannot fall because our Lord is within us and around us. Kris and I want to thank you for all your prayers. The Lord has heard them. His answer now is: "Come home my child to your heavenly rest." With that confidence in our Lord we can "Be Still." For those of you receiving this, as Kris said yesterday, this should really be a time to rejoice because heaven is near. Even with tears in our eyes, we ask you to join us in rejoicing in the gift of faith and the gift of heaven given to us by our Savior. Several weeks ago, I shared a sermon in which I talked to the graduates not about saying, "Good luck," but rather, "The Lord's blessings be with you." Kris and I wish you not good luck, but we wish you all the Lord's blessings, as you have been a blessing to us. I know many would love to visit with Kris, but please realize that as Kris has strength she will want to visit with her family first. You can always call me on my cell phone and you will not have to worry about waking up Kris. As we have opportunity, we will share with you our journey of faith in Tomahawk. In Christ, Mark and Kris

DAY 38:

Your Journey

**"I have brought you glory on earth by completing
the work you gave me to do."
JOHN 17:4**

T he word *tetelestai* was the Greek word Jesus uttered from the cross. It was the shout of victory. Yet, these words from John 17 were spoken by Jesus the night before he died. How could Jesus say that he had finished the work if he had not yet been crucified? These words come from Jesus' prayer in the upper room. As Jesus prays for himself, he knows that his sacrifice will be complete and that his work is as good as done.

Early in my parents' marriage, my father developed some serious ulcers. Through some mistreatment, the situation grew worse, and he ended up going to Marshfield. Extensive surgery followed to remove part of his back and stomach. For a young couple just starting out, the medical bills were quite enormous. They would pay some each month, knowing that it would take them a long time to pay off their bills. One day, they received a letter in the mail. "Mr. and Mrs. Orville Gass, your bill of $5,000 has been paid in full." Who did this for them? To this day, we still do not know who paid off their debt. But this is an example of *tetelestai*—to be finished; that is, to be paid in full.

You and I have been diagnosed with the most serious disease of all—sin. This sin, left untreated, would lead to death. Every time we sin, it is like adding on to the bill we owe God. He expects perfect holiness, with no sin, and we offer just the opposite. Our bill keeps mounting. We may try to pay it off, but we find that we can never catch up.

From the cross, when our dear Lord uttered those words of triumph, it was his stamping our bill with the words "Paid in Full!" The debt is paid in full! When He gave Himself on the cross, Jesus fully met the righteous demands of a holy law; He paid our debt in full. None of the Old Testament sacrifices could take away sins; their blood only covered sin. But the Lamb of God shed His blood, and that blood can take away the sins of the world.

Think about how Jesus must have felt on the cross. Was he sorrowful? Yes—he was in pain. But I have to believe that our Savior was also filled with an inexpressible joy because he had completed the sacrifice for the sins of all people. The work of salvation was complete.

Oh, perfect life of love! All, all is finished now,
All that he left his throne above To do for us below.

In perfect love He dies; For me he dies for me!
O all-atoning sacrifice, You died to make me free. (CW 138)

DAY 39:

Our Journey

June 24, 2005

Dear Friends in Christ,

I thought that I might send an update every Friday. So here goes. As I was working outside last night, I was wondering what people think when they drive by our house. What are their thoughts if they know us? Do they feel sorry for us? Do they think about death? Do they say a prayer? In a book given to us by the hospice nurse, I was reading a section that talked about the caregivers. It was comparing birth and death. In birth, the caregivers are helping to ensure a healthy transition into this world. In death, caregivers are really to help in the transition from this world to our heavenly home. That is what is taking place in our home. As we stand beside Kris, we are encouraging her and comforting her in her transition from this vale of tears to the glorious home in heaven. That is not something to feel sorry for. Our whole family has talked openly about what is happening and what is to take place. This past week, we have had several devotions on the home to come. We have met with the hospice nurse. Kris's attitude is awesome as she prepares to depart this world. Her attitude is the same as in life—acceptance of what the Lord is giving her. She even has begun to prepare items for her funeral. She invited our organist to come over and selected hymns. She asked me to have the funeral director come over to our house, and there was a peaceful resolve as she discussed with us the details of her funeral. At the beginning of the week, Kris was growing weaker, but the last couple of days, although still growing weaker, the rate of growing weaker has diminished. She seems to be somewhat stabilizing for the moment. Is it possible that she may have enough strength to join us for worship this weekend? Not sure, but we pray for that. We wish to thank all who so wondrously remembered us in your prayers and your notes. We can't possibly begin to mention each by name or to respond personally. But know that we truly appreciate every expression of love and support. When people drive by our home or when you think of it, we pray that you don't feel sorry for us but rejoice because we are experiencing life to its fullness. Jesus prayed the night before he died: "Now this is eternal life: that they may know you, the only true God, and Jesus Christ, whom you have sent." We know our Lord and so we have life and have it to its fullness. Sorrow and grief are not to be the attitude of our home, but victory and joy through our Lord Jesus Christ. Every day I pray that our home is not one of gloom, but of joy and laughter because nothing has defeated us, not even cancer. No, the cancer may think it is winning, but in the end, the victorious life for Kris awaits her. God's Blessings this weekend. Talk to you again next Friday. Mark and Kris

DAY 39:

Your Journey

"Day after day every priest stands and performs his religious duties; again and again he offers the same sacrifices, which can never take away sins. But when this priest had offered for all time one sacrifice for sins, he sat down at the right hand of God."
HEBREWS 10:11-13

The temple in the Old Testament was a very bloody place. Every morning and night, the priests would take bulls, cows or sheep and burn them up completely on the altar. Every day, the temple was permeated by the smell of death—the smell of blood.

I would imagine that Calvary had that same smell, since it was often used for crucifixions. All who passed by that place on Good Friday saw the three men on the cross, and they saw death in action. Their senses were filled with the sights, sounds and smells of the gruesome taking of life. But all this was to fulfill what the Lord had promised. In the Garden of Eden, shortly after Adam and Eve sinned, our gracious God promised that a "seed of the woman" would crush Satan. Throughout the whole Old Testament, one promise after another was given. God's people waited for their salvation to be *tetelestai*—to be finished. Day after day, the priests would sacrifice animals. When a priest examined an animal sacrifice and found it faultless, this word would apply—*tetelestai*. But none of those animals were spotless enough.

Jesus, of course, is the perfect Lamb of God, without spot or blemish. Christ satisfied God's justice by dying for all to pay for the sins of the believers. These sins can never be punished again, since that would violate God's justice. Sins can only be punished once, either by a substitute or by yourself.

When an artist completes a picture, or a writer a manuscript, he or she might say, "It is finished!" The death of Jesus on the cross "completes the picture" that God had been painting, the story that He had been writing for centuries. Because of the cross, we understand the ceremonies and prophecies of the Old Testament.

Christ, the obedient Servant, had finished the work the Father gave Him to do. Christ willingly and deliberately gave up His life; He laid down His life for His friends. *Tetelestai*—"It is forever done."

Not all the blood of beasts On Israel's altars slain
Could give the guilty conscience peace Or wash away the stain.

But Christ, the heav'nly Lamb, Takes all our sins away,
A sacrifice of nobler name And richer blood than they. (CW 128)

DAY 40:

Our Journey

July 1, 2005

Dear Friends in Christ,

While running along the river this morning, an eagle soared overhead for about ½ mile. Then it slowly picked up speed and moved on ahead until I could no longer see it. It reminded me of one of our favorite hymns, "On Eagles' Wings," which Kris has also chosen as one of her hymns for her funeral. How effortlessly that eagle soared above me while I exerted energy to keep my legs moving and my heart was pounding. This life is an effort—exerting energy to keep going—but how effortlessly our Savior God can lift us up. Right now, we are permitted to run beside Kris on this journey of faith while the heavenly Father lifts her up, but soon the Lord will take her on ahead of us, soaring to the heights of our heavenly home. When will that be? This past week has seen a certain amount of stability. We have settled into a routine which is comfortable for Kris. Some days she has more energy than others. Some days I think that the Lord could come soon, while at other times I think that she may continue on here for several months. This all serves to remind us that "our time is in your hands, O Lord." Although somewhat weaker, Kris continues to maintain a certain level of comfort. We are so grateful for the letters and e-mails of encouragement. I read them to her as they come in every day. There have been some awesome letters and notes of encouragement for us. As Kris and I have discussed, these notes would never have been realized if we did not decide to share our journey with you. I believe that the Lord has also used us to give others the opportunity to let their faith shine. We cannot even begin to adequately thank you all for your prayers. Please accept this meager attempt to say thanks as acknowledgement that your support is greatly appreciated. Besides that, nothing new to report. We wish all of you a blessed 4th of July weekend. What a blessing to be not only Americans—but Christian Americans. Talk to you next Friday. Until then, God's Blessings. Mark and Kris

DAY 40:

Your Journey

"Be still before the Lord, all mankind, because he has roused
himself from his holy dwelling. Then he showed me Joshua the high
priest standing before the angel of the Lord, and Satan standing
at his right side to accuse him. The Lord said to Satan, 'The Lord
rebuke you, Satan! The Lord, who has chosen Jerusalem, rebuke
you! Is not this man a burning stick snatched from the fire?'"

ZECHARIAH 2:13–3:2

In the word before us for today, Zechariah uses the image of our Lord as a great King who decides to leave his throne. Why? Sharp accusations have been made, and now it is time to act.

When we feel uncertain in life, it is because Satan is right there accusing us. "Have you really done enough to earn God's love?" "How could God love you?" "Your life is a mess—God certainly has left you—you are all alone." "Your sickness, your trouble in life is a result of your own sin." "God is punishing you." Satan whispers these and many other accusations in our ears. But notice what the Lord does. He rebukes Satan. He rebukes Satan because he has chosen Jerusalem for himself.

Jerusalem is us—His Holy Christian Church, His family of believers. Remember the saying, "Snatching victory from the jaws of defeat." God calls us a "burning stick snatched from the fire." Yes, at times it may seem that our lives are on fire. About 3 p.m. on Good Friday, it seemed that our Lord's life was "on fire"—that is, that he was in the jaws of defeat. But the outcome was never in doubt.

In the same way, our lives seem to be "on fire." Defeat may seem to loom in front of us. It is especially at these times that you and I need to "be still" before the Lord, so that we can hear again his victory cry. Put aside the wailing and complaining in life and look closely at the cross. As Jesus says *tetelestai*—"It is finished"—we see Jesus home victorious. There is the Savior who has rescued us from all the battles of life. Because of Him, we can look at any uncertainty in life and think to ourselves: "*Tetelestai*—It is finished. My Savior has completed everything for me. He has completed my salvation. He has my home in heaven waiting for me. He has battled all for me. I need not fear but rest in the stillness of knowing that all is now done—BY HIM!" As his head begins to sink in death, let your head rise up with joy and peace and security. Why? *Tetelestai*—It is finished!

Be still, my soul, the Lord is on your side. Bear patiently times of uncertainty. When doubts sneak in and threaten to devour Our blissful hope of life eternally. Upon his shoulders all our sins were heavy, "It is finished," the payment is complete.

(Modified verse from CW 415)

DAY 41:

Our Journey

July 8, 2005 – Morning Update

Dear Friends in Christ,

Do we ever ask the question, "Why?" Of course we do. We wouldn't be human if didn't. But our prayer has not been so much of why this cancer, but why this pain. As the cancer continues to grow, it is beginning to cause Kris pain and weariness of body. I often plead with the Lord that Kris would not suffer too much pain. I wonder why should she. Oh, sure, she is a sinner, and she has her faults. However, why not me? Why can't I take this pain instead of her—why shouldn't I. My sins are far more grievous. Ask any of her friends, and they will say that growing up she was the classic good girl. I would not be the pastor I am today without her. She is the greatest conversationalist, and I learned much from her. So why not me instead of her? I'm sure you are wondering if we are beginning to slip. Are they doubting? No, but you who have traveled this journey with us in prayer know that our faith and confidence is in the Lord. Many have written letters of encouragement as well as thanks for the expression of faith. Yet, we must remember not to look to ourselves or even to our own faith—rather, our faith points us the Lord. This was impressed upon me about 4:00 this morning. Kris was up, and the pain was beginning to act up again. I went to retrieve her medicine. We all realize what it is like to function at 4 in the morning, especially when we had been up at midnight and 2 a.m. I walked in by Kris and opened the medicine bottle and grabbed the wrong one. I had grabbed our "spiritual medicine bottle." Whenever anyone is sick in our congregation I give them a medicine bottle, but inside are Bible passages on little sheets of paper. "Take one daily and more when needed." We cannot overdose on this medicine. Pulling out the first card was this passage: "Peace I leave with you; my peace I give you. I do not give to you as

172

the world gives. Do not let your hearts be troubled and do not be afraid" (John 14). There it is. In the midst of the pain of life is sure peace. That peace is conferred upon us by the great gift of our Lord. I read that passage to Kris and was reminded that our Lord calms our hearts with the message of his love. This past week saw some great ups for Kris. In some respects, she is holding her own. Several sisters and mother and cousin and niece visited with her. They had some wonderful times with her and some laughs and memories to share. Over the last two days, she has been very tired and pain does increase. Also, walking last night was becoming difficult. Yet, her spirit is the same, and one moment she is laughing with me and the next she is telling me what to do—nothing's changed there. This weekend, her family will all be gathering for the McPeak family reunion in New London. Although we can't be there, yet we will be there in spirit. Once again, thank you for all the cards and letters of encouragement. They are wonderful gifts of inspiration, and I read each one to Kris. She enjoys them all. I have been wanting to send out some Thank Yous, but energy and time do not permit it. Please know that each note is truly appreciated. God's Blessings, and we will talk again next week. Until then, remember that we live in the sure and living peace of our Lord. Mark and Kris

DAY 41:

Your Journey

"For it is by grace you have been saved, through
faith—and this not from yourselves,
it is a gift of God—not by works, so that no one can boast."
EPHESIANS: 2:8-9

There was once a rather eccentric evangelist named Alexander Wooten, who was approached by a flippant young man who asked, "What must I do to be saved?" "It's too late!" Wooten replied, and went about his work. The young man became alarmed. "Do you mean that it's too late for me to be saved?" he asked. "Is there nothing I can do?" "Too late!" said Wooten. "It's already been done! The only thing you can do is believe."

Imagine the Lord saying to you, "It is too late! There is nothing you can do to be saved." In effect, that is what our Lord is saying to us right now in this great letter to the Ephesians. There is nothing you can do. In fact, when the preacher above said, "The only thing you can do is believe," he made an unfortunate word choice. Even our faith is not something we do.

Look closely at the beautiful words of this passage. First comes the word "grace." Grace is such a huge word! It is God's undeserved love for sinners. I recently read a devotion in which the writer spoke of grace in this way: When we ran away from our Lord, he ran faster to catch us. If I see my child running from the house toward the street, where there is a truck speeding around the corner, what am I going to do? I am going to run after my child faster than my child is running away from me. Why? Because I love my child. Even though my child is disobeying my command to never go into the road, I am not going to say, "Go ahead—get hit by the truck because that is what you deserve since you are disobeying me." Instead, I am going to expend all

174

of my energy to reach my child before he or she reaches the road. On an even greater level, this is what our Lord has done for us. How many times we have raced away from him, and yet he races even faster after us. He expended his energy on the cross so that we could be rescued. Why? Because he loves us. That's grace.

But then how do we receive that love? That's faith. And how do we get faith? The passage above reminds us—"it is a gift from God." Faith is a gift, and through this gift, we receive all the other gifts of love from our God. Jesus once told his disciples that our faith is to be like that of a little child.

Six months after our wedding, my wife had a miscarriage. This happened in the middle of the night. She needed to remain in the hospital for several days. The morning after the miscarriage, I went home to pick up my oldest daughter, who was about seven at the time. On the way to the hospital, I explained to her as simply as I could what had happened. Obviously, this was a traumatic time for us. Immediately, these words came from my daughter's mouth: "Don't be sad, Dad, God has a plan for all this." Wow! From the mouth of babes we are often taught great lessons in life. This girl had no idea of the big picture at that time. But she didn't need it. She had been taught that her Savior has won the victory on the cross, and that he is in control of everything—simply that the Savior loves us. That's all she needed to know. As adults, our minds often get in the way, and we want to know all the answers. Instead, let Ephesians 2, let our Lord's word from the cross—*tetelestai*—and let our Lord's love be enough for us to say: "God has a plan." Rest in the stillness of knowing that our Lord's plan for us is centered in his grace.

Amazing grace—how sweet the sound—That saved a wretch like me!
I once was lost but now am found, Was blind but now I see. (CW 379)

DAY 42:

Our Journey

July 8, 2005 – Evening Update

Dear Friends in Christ,

As I sat here watching Kris sleep, the clarion of our church began playing "What a Friend We Have in Jesus." I am prompted to let you know what has transpired today. As I wrote this morning, I kept thinking that Kris is sleeping a long time. When she finally awoke around 9 a.m., she could not get out of bed. In fact, she was not very responsive. She could sit on the edge of the bed, but very weakly. What was happening? This ran through my head. She also had a temp of 103. Apparently, there are such things as tumor fevers. At 11 a.m., she could hardly lift her legs. However, God in his great mercy gathered her strength, and at 2 p.m., she was ever so weakly able to take a walk to the bathroom and back. So she has rebounded somewhat. However, she is in a much weakened state. There have been many times when Kris bounced back, but it seems there is not much bounce left. It seems that the door to heaven is closer now for Kris. Seeing that door come closer provides both joy and sorrow. Yet, my girls and I are saddened more by the pain that Kris might have to endure. I know you have, but this weekend please ask our gracious Lord to hold his dear Lamb close to his face and calm her heart and her body. Last weekend, I was supposed to perform a wedding, which I had to bow out of. This weekend, we have two weddings, which I probably will not make. But, for Kris, there is the greater wedding, as she will soon sit at the wedding feast of the Lamb and receive all the blessings from his sacrifice for us. A good friend of mine reminded me tonight that God did not promise us every earthly blessing, but he did promise us eternal life with him, as well as promising that he will walk with us here. As the situation warrants, I will probably not wait until Friday but will update as needed. God's Blessings. Mark and Kris

DAY 42:

Your Journey

"And he died for all, that those who live
should no longer live for themselves
but for him who died for them and was raised again."
2 Corinthians 5:15

Wednesday of Holy Week is often called Silent Wednesday. Nothing is recorded about what our Lord did that day. One can well imagine that our Lord spent some time in prayer and meditation that day as he prepared for the beginning of his suffering and death. It would also be good for us to spend some time below the cross meditating on the suffering of our Lord.

Christ's death means that there is a change in our lives. We no longer live for ourselves but for him who died for us. When Christ cried out on the cross, "It is finished," victory over sin was won. Nothing is required of us for our salvation. To show our gratefulness, however, our response should be, "Thank you, Lord, for giving your life for me. Now I want to live for You and serve You till the end of my days."

This was the reaction of Frances Havergal, known as the "consecration poet," whose life was characterized by simple faith. Once, while visiting an art museum in Dusseldorf, Germany, she was moved by a vivid painting of Christ wearing His crown of thorns as He stood before Pilate and the mob. Under the painting by Sternberg were the words, "This have I done for thee; what hast thou done for Me?" As Havergal gazed at the painting in tears, she scribbled down the lines of the hymn below on a scrap of paper. After returning to her home in England, she felt the poetry was so poor that she tossed the lines into a stove. The scorched scrap of paper amazingly floated out of the flames and landed on the floor, where it was found by her father,

Rev. William Havergal, an Anglican minister, a noted poet, and a church musician. He encouraged her to preserve the poem by composing the first melody for it.

From the scorched areas of our lives, there floats for us a beautiful picture. Yes, it is an ugly scene—a scene of death, crucifixion, taunting and mocking—but it is beautiful to us because there we see the full extent of our Lord's love. Over the next few days, take time to view this great scene. With Francis Havergal, let us also sing:

I gave my life for thee; My precious blood I shed
That thou might'st ransomed be And quickened from the dead.
I gave my life for thee; Come, give thyself to me!

I suffered much for thee, More than my tongue may tell,
Of bitt'rest agony, To rescue thee from hell.
I suffered much for thee; Come, bear they cross with me.

And I have brought to thee, Down from my home above
Salvation full and free, My pardon and my love;
Great gifts I brought for thee; Come, bring they gifts to me. (CW 454)

DAY 43:

Our Journey

July 12, 2005

Dear Friends in Christ,

As I sit here by the kitchen counter, I can now look over at Kris as she lies in her hospital bed. Yesterday, we took her out of her bed and brought her into the middle of our dining room to remain around us for the last few hours she has left on this earth. Heaven's door is close now. But let me tell you about an interesting conversation I had with my eight-year-old, Kayla. "Daddy, why are mom's eyes black around them?" "You know what is happening to mom, right?" I responded. "Yes, she is getter sicker?" "That's right, Kayla, and then what will happen?" "She will die." "Then what will happen, Kayla?" "She will go home to heaven to be with Jesus?" "You are right, Kayla, and the black around her eyes is just how people look as they are getting ready to leave to go home to heaven." "But when she gets to heaven," Kayla began to laugh and continued, "she can't sit in the front row because Tony said he wanted to sit there." Our good friend Tony had told me to tell Kris that when she gets to heaven she can sit anywhere but in the front row because he wants to sit there. The faith of a child—amongst the sadness there is that joy and happiness because she believes her mom is going to heaven and will not have to suffer any more. How many people have often commented about how hard it must be for our daughters. Maybe not as hard as one thinks, because the Lord has given each a wonderful trust in Jesus. Their mom has also given them courage and strength. I refuse to let our home be turned into a morgue. No, we have the privilege of carrying Kris to heaven's door. The sadness is not for her but for those left behind. Even then, we are not alone, because the great shepherd who holds Kris so close is also holding us. Having Kris right here now in the middle of our lives means that we can cry and laugh at the same time. Sadness and joy are mixed together to provide a time of love and hope and closeness. Kris seems to be resting comfortably now. Asleep most of the time, I watch as from time to time each person walking by stops and leans over to speak to Kris or we talk about what she wants us to do or we stand and pray. It has been said that in the midst of life there is death. The opposite is also true, in the midst of death there is life and life to the fullest with Jesus by our side. I often stop and speak to Kris about heaven and the joys that await her—about seeing loved ones gone on before—but more importantly, about seeing Jesus. I often think that the best part of heaven will be that we can look straight into the eyes of our loving Savior. Right now, we wait for Kris to open her eyes so that we can see them shining out at us one more time. But how awesome to see those lovely eyes of our gracious Savior shining down on us for the first time! It has got to give us goose bumps for eternity! Well, I just wanted to share with you where we are on our journey. I can't even begin to thank each person for your thoughts and your prayers and your wonderful words of encouragement. I have read everything I have received up until yesterday to Kris. I know she hears them. God's blessings this day. When you think of us this day, don't think so much of sadness as of the joy of heaven, and pray that you yourself are on the path that leads to our heavenly joy. Mark and Kris

DAY 43:

Your Journey

"My command is this: Love each other as I have loved you."
JOHN 15:12

Oftentimes, on the night before our Lord died, we focus just on the Lord's Supper or on the betrayal in the Garden. But our Lord spoke many things to his disciples on this evening. In the middle of his last instructions before his death, our Lord gave the disciples a new command: "Love one another." Wait a moment! This isn't new! We have been told throughout Scripture to love one another. That is true. But the reason this command is new is because now this command was to be based on what Jesus was about to do. Notice he says, "Love each other AS I HAVE LOVED YOU."

This love is first of all modeled by our Lord. That night in the upper room, our Lord got down on his hands and knees and washed the feet of his disciples. Let me tell you, it is not easy to wash the feet of a perfectly healthy fellow human being. One night during a Lenten meditation, I called a man to the front and had him sit in a chair. In front of the whole congregation, I—the pastor—got down and took off his shoes and socks, put his feet in water and washed them. I have to admit that I felt awkward and somewhat degraded doing this. But look at our Lord. Here we have the Creator of the whole universe—the God who has all majesty and splendor—getting down and washing the feet of his sinful creatures. What love! But this love reaches its greatest model when Christ climbs up on the cross willingly for us. Here we have the Creator of the whole universe—the God who has all majesty and splendor—willingly allowing himself to suffer one of the most gruesome and cruel deaths ever devised by sinful mankind.

This is the love that we need to examine and meditate upon. There is a hymn that leads us in quiet contemplation of our Lord's love. "O Sacred Head, Now Wounded" was part of the final portion of a lengthy poem that addressed the various parts of Christ's body as He suffered on the cross. It is difficult to join our fellow believers each Lenten season in the singing of this passion hymn without being moved almost to tears. For more than 800 years, these worshipful lines from the heart of a devoted medieval monk have portrayed for parishioners a memorable view of the suffering Savior.

> *O sacred head, now wounded, With grief and shame weighed down,*
> *Now scornfully surrounded, With thorns your only crown,*
> *O sacred head, no glory Now from your face does shine;*
> *Yet, though despised and gory, I joy to call you mine.*
>
> *What language shall I borrow To thank you, dearest Friend,*
> *For this, your dying sorrow, Your pity without end?*
> *Oh, make me yours forever, And keep me strong and true;*
> *Lord, let me never, never Outlive my love for you. (CW 105)*

The Conclusion

Be Still in the Midst of Life's Ending

The devotion for "Your Journey" will lead us from the words of Jesus from the cross, "Father, into Your Hands I commit my Spirit" to encourage us to Be Still even at the end of our earthly lives.

DAY 44:

Our Journey

July 13, 2005

Dear Friends in Christ,
There are these lines of my favorite Easter hymn:

> **"The foe was triumphant when on Calvary,**
> **The Lord of creation was nailed to the tree.**
> **In Satan's domain did the hosts shout and jeer,**
> **For Jesus was slain, whom the evil ones fear.**
>
> **But short was their triumph; the Savior arose,**
> **And death hell and Satan he vanquished, his foes.**
> **The conquering Lord lifts his banner on high;**
> **He lives, yes, lives and will nevermore die."**

I often think of cancer in the same way. Cancer was laughing and jeering. It was surging forth thinking that it had defeated Kris. It was ready to claim another victory. But, just then, our dearest Lord snatched victory away. That evil cancer was turned on its head as the Lord just simply used this disease to proclaim his glory—to share the good news of peace through Jesus and to rescue another child from this world. This took place during Kris's lifetime, as I am convinced that there will be people in heaven who were strengthened by Kris's example of faith. And then there remained nothing but sweet rest in the heavenly home. This morning, our Lord said to Kris, "Enough my child. You have suffered enough. Your journey is over. Look, I am opening the door to heaven. Come on in—here, you are so weak, but let me carry you through the door, and look around you. Look at the glory I have prepared for you. Look, here is your room that I have prepared. Over there—do you see them, there is your father and your sisters and all the other loved ones. There is Abraham and Moses, but most importantly, there is your heavenly Father. Go ahead, he is waiting for you—Go climb up on his lap and let him give you the hug of eternity." For we who are left behind, the door has closed, but not for long. We who have walked with Kris to heaven's door know that our journey continues. So ends this chapter of our journey together. Our family has been strengthened by the many e-mails, cards and words given to us. Now, what remains is the glorious celebration of victory. That will take place this coming Sunday. We will have visitation at our church, Redeemer Lutheran in Tomahawk, on Saturday night from 3-8 p.m., with a prayer service at 7:45 p.m. We will then have more time of visitation on Sunday from 12-4, with the service of life and victory at 4 p.m. To accommodate as many people as possible, we will hold this service of victory at Tomahawk Public High School Auditorium. A meal will follow in the commons. There will also be a time of fellowship at the Comfort Inn. For those who may travel for this, we have secured a special rate at the Comfort Inn, and we invite all to join us. We especially invite our many brothers in the ministry and ask that you will sing several hymns as a group. One last word: for those of you who have walked with us for so long, if there is any one lesson to take from all this, it is certainly not bitterness or resentment. Not if we truly can imagine the glory of heaven. Rather, Kris's journey ought to remind us that we are all just on our journey of faith. That journey of faith can only be traveled one way—that is by faith in Jesus. Turn to him, and may he guide you and us through this life to our heavenly home. God's Blessings, my dear friends. Mark and Kris

DAY 44:

Your Journey

> "Jesus called out with a loud voice, 'Father,
> into your hands I commit my spirit.'
> When he had said this, he breathed his last."
> LUKE 23:46

During this journey, we have gone a long way with Jesus. In many ways, our journey—your journey—followed the suffering of our Savior. We went with him to Gethsemane and watched his agony. We followed him to the court of the High Priest and observed his patience. We went with him to Pilate and saw him condemned for no sin at all. We followed him to Calvary, where, in spite of the cruelty and agony, we heard him pray for his enemies, guarantee the penitent thief a place in heaven, and finally cry out after six hours of excruciating agony on the cross, "It is finished." Now he is about to breathe his last.

How does our Lord face death? When life's ending stares him in the face, what is the emotion that fills his heart? Fear? Absolutely not. There now remains for Jesus only confidence and trust. Did you notice how our Lord spoke his last words? The Bible says that he did so with "a loud voice." There was no timidity here! There was no uncertainty! With the confidence that welled up in his soul and gave him the strength to literally shout it out, he placed himself in the hands of his Father.

Let's be blunt—how do you feel about death? Some people don't like to talk about death. Some time ago, I had a lady ask me not to use the word death. Instead, she wanted me to say "passed away" or "expired." But as the psalmist says, "In the midst of life we are in death." Death is unfortunately part of this life. But death is enough to bring fear to the heart of the unbeliever. An anonymous unbelieving queen cried out as she was about to die, "My kingdom for one minute of time." According to some reports, when King Louis of France, who had massacred the Huguenots in cold blood on St. Bartholomew's night, was about to die, he became so frightened and terrified that he perspired drops of blood.

At the opposite end of the spectrum, I have had the privilege of being by the side of many Christians as they are about to breathe their last. Is the Christian anxious in the face of death? Of course Christians have those moments. We are all human, after all. But, one by one, I have seen Christians slip into the greatest stillness of all—complete confidence and trust in the Lord in the face of life's ending. Why? They know the gracious promises of love given by our Lord through his death on the cross.

In January 2001, I had the privilege of being with my father during his last moments. All of us children were gathered around his bed. My last words to my father were: "Go home, Dad, and we will not be far behind." Then it was as if we ushered him to the very gates of heaven and watched him slip inside. Someday, we will all face death. How we face death is dependent upon our relationship with our Savior today. Look up at the cross. See our Lord's immense love. Be filled with his good and gracious promises. Then, when life's ending—death—stares you in the face, you can also be still and place yourself into the hands of your heavenly Father.

> *I fall asleep in Jesus' wounds; There pardon for my sin abounds.*
> *Yea, Jesus' blood and righteousness My beauty are, my glorious dress.*
> *In these before my God I'll stand When I shall reach my heavenly land.*

> *In peace and joy I now depart; God's child I am with all my heart.*
> *I thank you, death, for leading me To that true life, where I would be.*
> *So cleansed by Christ, I fear not death. Lord Jesus, strengthen now my faith. (CW 608)*

DAY 45:

End of our Journey

Just in Time to
Live in God's Stillness

I would like to close our journey together with the message I shared with my congregation the first Sunday I was back in worship after our 42-day journey in the hospital following Kris's brain surgery in 2004. May this final word help you to live in the stillness of our Lord!

Galatians 4:4-7; 6: 2, 10 "But when the time had fully come, God sent his Son, born of a woman, born under law, to redeem those under law, that we might receive the full rights of sons. Because you are sons, God sent the Spirit of his Son into our hearts, the Spirit who calls out, '*Abba*, Father.' So you are no longer a slave, but a son; and since you are a son, God has made you also an heir. Carry each other's burdens, and in this way you will fulfill the law of Christ. Therefore, as we have opportunity, let us do good to all people, especially to those who belong to the family of believers."

Dear Brothers and Sisters in Christ,

It is good to be back! Wow! Is it good to be back! It has been over 50 days since I last stood before you and was privileged to share God's Word with you. I am now back, and today I would like to share a special message for you from God's Word. While in the hospital, Kris and I received numerous cards and expressions of love and support. But one card intrigued me—not because it was filled with a very generous expression of support, but because of the name: Justin Thyme—J u s t i n T h y m e—Justin Thyme. For the life of me I could not think of who Justin Thyme was. He wasn't in the Tomahawk phone book, although I knew the card was from Tomahawk. He wasn't a friend of ours or our children and did not have children enrolled in our learning center. Who was Justin Thyme? While inquiring about this with my daughter, I must have said it a particular way because she told me to slow down how I said it: Justin Thyme—Just in Thyme—Just in Time. Someone or some group of people were sending their expressions of support "Just in Time." Actually, throughout our 42 days at the hospital, there were a number of things that happened, "Just in Time." These were not coincidences, but were part of God's great plan, which he worked out "Just in Time." This is not necessarily going to be a typical sermon, but rather a message of love recounting how God was with us through these past 42 days and worked it out "Just in Time."

In order to fully understand how all things worked out "Just in Time," the first part of our Scripture passage takes us all the way back some 2,000 years ago. Really, we need to go farther back to see that Kris's battle with cancer did not just begin suddenly. No, actually, we go way back some 6,000 years to that initial battle that took place in the Garden of Eden. After Adam and Eve turned their backs on their loving Creator and chose to follow their own path, our God stepped in "just in time" and promised the coming of the Savior. But despite that first promise of the Savior, sin and imperfection had already entered this world and along with it, disease and sickness, sorrow and tears. Kris's battle with cancer began then. Your battle, your trials, every obstacle that we all face in life began then.

Some 4,000 years later, after all of the prophecies and promises, our passage says, "When the time had fully come." In other words, at "just the right time—just in time," our Heavenly Father said to his son, "Now is the time to step into this world and take on human form—now is the time to live amongst these humans who would rather not love us—now is the time to show the full extent of our love for them. It is time for you to work out the plan of salvation." Down to this earth our Savior came, born of the virgin Mary, wandering around Palestine to preach the good news and allowing humans to mock him, beat him, scourge him and, finally, crucify him. On that cross, Jesus faced every trial, temptation, every punishment for us. Kris's deliverance from her battle against cancer began there on the cross and there at the empty tomb. Your deliverance and shelter from all trial and trouble begins at the cross and the empty tomb.

These past 40+ days have been unique not in the sense that this was a problem unknown to so many others. What makes this unique is how we can see God working out his plan for us "just in time." Over a year ago, God brought to our congregation the unique opportunity to have a congregational evangelist. After a year of training, Kevin was ready; in fact, it was "just in time" for him to step forward while I needed to be absent. Who would have seen this except our loving Lord of the church, who still wanted his family of believers shepherded in my absence? Many of you know how we joked about our daughter Katie having to move back home in January to wait until she found a job or that our daughter Kimberly just received her driver's license. But now we see how these happened "just in time" so that our family could continue to maintain their daily lives while we needed to be gone.

While driving home from Kris's first CAT scan back in early February, my plan was to drop her off at Wittenberg, where we had a car waiting for her, while I headed over to Sheboygan for meetings. We were just transferring her into her vehicle at Wittenberg when the doctor called "just in time" so that we could hear the news together and be there to support each other. Even in small details, our Lord is in control. Following the surgery, when Kris's brain pressure began to swell, the physician arrived "just in time" to put Kris into the coma so as to prevent harm or injury to her brain.

Now we come to the second part of our passages. Paul, after reminding Christians about the basic foundations of our faith, encourages our response to God's love. When others are caught in a sin or temptation or even a trial, we are encouraged to "carry each other's burdens." Some of you may remember that one day while I was taking a little rest in the CCU waiting room, I dreamed that I was sitting on one of the couches and behind me was this large crowd of people—some I knew and some I didn't. I believe that was a picture of all those who were praying for Kris. Paul further says, "Therefore, as we have opportunity, let us do good to all people, especially to those who belong to the family of believers." Here—do you see these—two grocery bags full of cards, many of them from you. These are expressions of love born from your faith in Jesus. You have come to know that God saved you "just in time." "Just in time" Jesus came for us. And now, "just in time," you were there for one of your fellow believers. It was unbelievable the number of my brothers in the ministry who stopped by to share God's comfort. It was wonderful to see so many friends—so many of you who wrote to share God's comfort with us. It was "just in time."

Other things happened that were "just in time." Especially, while Kris was sleeping, I had the privilege to meet many people who were also in the waiting room of the CCU standing vigil over their loved ones. While I was there, two families asked me to share God's Word with their loved one before they died. One family in particular became friends, and they are now often in my prayers. I praise God that I could be there "just in time" to bring them God's Word. There was one group that came in near the end of Kris's stay in CCU. Their loved one was just being put into a coma. I saw the look in their eyes—the same look I felt in my eyes the night of the 14th when the doctor put Kris in her coma. But there is something I didn't see in their eyes. They had very little hope—that is, hope in the Lord. They had left the church and God some time ago. I took them to the Word and to the psalms. I praise God that they came "just in time" before Kris left CCU so that I could share God's Word with them. Several days later, I came down to see how they were doing and I came in on one of them as they were reading one of the psalms I had mentioned. It is possible that this all happened "just in time" so that they could hear the Word.

There are so many other incidents that are tucked away in the back of my mind—too many to consider. The doctors were very concerned about Kris, and by the end of the second week were leaning toward putting in a trach and feeding tube. But Kris woke up "just in time" so she did not have to go through that. While in rehab, she passed her swallow test "just in time" so that we did not have to come home on a special diet. We have now come home "just in time" so that we could be with you for Holy Week and Easter.

"Just in time." When we look back over all of this, we can see that it was more than "just in time." It was "just in God's time." God is not the author of evil, and so we do not blame him for these trials. These are our own fault because of our sinfulness and imperfection. Yet, in our weakness, we see God's strength. In our uncertainty, we see God's sure and gracious promises of love and protection. As I look back, I also see other opportunities that I had that I squandered because of lack of strength or desire. When we all look back over this chapter in our lives, what does it teach us? Does it not teach us first and foremost to keep our eyes focused on our Lord? Our doctors are wonderful gifts, but it was the Great Physician who caused this miraculous recovery. This experience teaches us to remember what our greatest gift is: our Lord and Savior. Sitting next a loved one in the CCU room, there was no comfort in the fact that we have three cars, that we live in a nice home, that we own a bunch of possessions. One's only comfort is the comfort that is always "just in time"—that our Lord came "just in time" to be our Savior, our Deliverer and our Friend. Our comfort is knowing that His coming "just in time" has secured for us that blessed privilege of being called "sons." We are sons and daughters of our Father in heaven, who always comes "just in time" to our need. One day, he will come "just in time" to deliver us from this world of trials and troubles and take us home to heaven. That's what the empty tomb teaches us. Just as yesterday, one of our members, Harriett Jones, who suffered so much in these past years, was delivered to be with her Lord forever in the glories of heaven. But not just for her, but for all, who by faith are children of God. Knowing this, it is our privilege to be present "just in time" to share that same love that we have received from our Lord. As we begin to wind down the Lenten season, let us rejoice that our Lord came "just in time," and I further thank the Lord that so many helped carry our burden "just in time."

I realize that there is not a Justin Thyme—J u s t i n T h y m e—in the phone book. But he exists. Now I know who he is—He is the Lord coming "just in time" with his love, and He is there sharing his love through your "just in time" expressions of love and support. Amen.

Made in the USA
Charleston, SC
25 January 2016